EVEN MORE
CHILDREN'S
MISCELLANY

NOTE TO READERS

EVEN MORE
^ CHILDREN'S
MISCELLANY

Smart, silly, and strange information
that's essential to know

By Guy Macdonald
Illustrated by Niki Catlow

chronicle books · san francisco

First published in the United States in 2008 by
Chronicle Books LLC.

Copyright © 2006 by Buster Books.
Originally published in Great Britain in 2006 by Buster Books, an
imprint of Michael O'Mara Books Limited.

Typeset in Langer.
Manufactured in China.

Library of Congress Cataloging-in-Publication Data available.
ISBN 978-0-8118-6251-6

10 9 8 7 6 5 4 3 2 1

Chronicle Books LLC
680 Second Street, San Francisco, California 94107

www.chroniclekids.com

CONTENTS

CONTENTS

CONTENTS

CONTENTS

CONTENTS

THINGS THERE SHOULD BE WORDS FOR THAT THERE AREN'T

The strangely pleasant feeling of desperately needing the toilet

The feeling of disappointment you get when you receive the same present twice

An itch that you can get rid of only by scratching another part of your body

The shock of hearing your own name spoken during a daydream in class

The extra-delicious taste that food has when you can have only one mouthful

The faraway feeling you get in your head when you read something out loud in front of lots of people

The love you feel for someone (usually a brother or sister) that can be expressed only by annoying them

The shame of being told off by a friend's parent

Outer space begins 62 miles (100 km) above Earth's surface. The line where outer space begins is called the Kármán line.

A BILLION AGO

A billion seconds ago, your parents were children.

A billion minutes ago, the Roman Empire was booming.

A billion hours ago, Neanderthals lived in Europe and Asia.

A billion months ago, dinosaurs ruled Earth.

A billion years ago, primitive life evolved.

———THE DIFFERENCE BETWEEN TANGERINES,——— SATSUMAS, CLEMENTINES, AND ORANGES

TANGERINE
Has dimpled skin that peels off easily. Smaller than an orange, but heavy for its size. The name comes from Tangier, a port in Morocco, from where the first tangerines were shipped to Europe.

SATSUMA
Sweet, seedless, and smaller than an orange. The skin can be peeled easily. First exported from Satsuma Province in Japan, where satsumas are called *mikan*.

CLEMENTINE
Smooth, glossy, vibrant orange skin that is thin and easy to peel. They separate easily into 8 to 12 juicy, sweet-tasting segments.

ORANGE
Thought to be a cross between a pomelo (a pale-green fruit bigger than a grapefruit) and a tangerine. (A grapefruit is a cross between a pomelo and an orange.)

MANDARIN ORANGE
Resembles an orange, but is shaped like a flattened sphere. It comes in several varieties, including the tangerine, satsuma, and clementine.

TANGOR
A cross between a mandarin and an orange. Thin, easy-to-peel rind and pale-orange pulp that tastes spicy and tart.

———THE LAYERS OF EARTH'S ATMOSPHERE———

Troposphere............................0 to 9 miles (0 to 14.5 km) above Earth

Stratosphere........................9 to 31 miles (14.5 to 50 km) above Earth

Mesosphere........................31 to 53 miles (50 to 85) km above Earth

Thermosphere............53 to 372 miles (85 to 600) km above Earth

Exosphere................................372 miles+ (600 km+) above Earth

SMELLY CHEESES

Vieux Boulogne
Pont l'Évêque
Munster
Camembert
Gammelost
Limburger
Brie de Meaux
Roquefort
Reblochon
Livarot
Banon
Gorgonzola
Époisses de Bourgogne
Stinking Bishop

REAL SONIC WEAPONS

Sonic weapons are weapons that use sound waves to deter or injure the enemy.

INFRASONIC SIREN
Modern cruise ships have experimented with infrasonic sirens to repel enemies at sea. The low-frequency sound can make concrete walls crumble and humans violently ill.

ANTI-FROGMAN WEAPON
A ship can sound its ordinary navigation sonar to deter enemy scuba divers. The sound waves disorient divers, who either panic and drown or are forced to the surface.

SONIC BULLETS
These high-power beams of ultrasound can measure up to 145 decibels. The sound waves stop people in their tracks.

INFRASONIC GUN
In the 1950s, the first infrasonic gun was immediately classified as "almost lethal" when it made the internal organs of the test subjects bleed. The gun made the laboratory shake violently, even on low power.

THINGS TO AVOID WHEN PLAYING IN THE OCEAN

Portuguese man-of-war......................Jellyfish with stinging tentacles

Stinging seaweed....................Venomous animal disguised as a plant

Fire coral............................Looks like coral but has stinging tentacles

Stonefish........................Looks like a stone but has poisonous spines

Sea urchin............Has poisonous spines that break off in your foot

Stingray.......................................Fish that lies in the sand and has a razor-sharp spine and stinging tail

Blue-ringed octopus...............The size of a tennis ball, with poison powerful enough to kill a human in minutes

INEXPENSIVE COLLECTIBLES

Chewing-gum packets • Airplane sick bags
Potato-chip bags • Rubber ducks • Matchboxes
Subway tickets • Four-leaf clovers • Fruit sticker-labels
Human teeth • Buttons • Ballpoint pens
Fridge magnets • Soft-drink cans

---PHASES OF THE MOON---

On average, the Moon takes 29½ days to complete one orbit around Earth. This is known as a lunar month. During this time, the Moon goes through a complete cycle, from new Moon to full Moon and back again. The phases are:

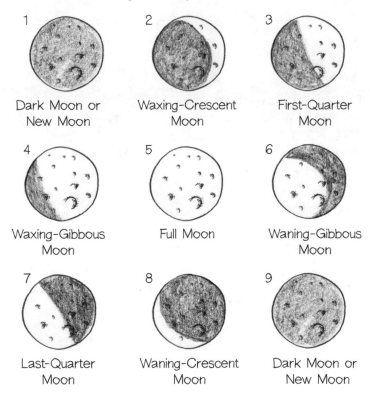

1 Dark Moon or New Moon

2 Waxing-Crescent Moon

3 First-Quarter Moon

4 Waxing-Gibbous Moon

5 Full Moon

6 Waning-Gibbous Moon

7 Last-Quarter Moon

8 Waning-Crescent Moon

9 Dark Moon or New Moon

In the Southern Hemisphere, the above is reversed so that a waxing-crescent Moon is seen as the left side of the Moon, and a waning-crescent Moon is seen as the right side of the Moon.

> Paraguay is the only country in the world whose national flag has two different sides.

POISONOUS PLANTS

Deadly nightshade • Hemlock
Holly • Death cap mushroom
Mistletoe • Iris • Yew

HOW TO KEEP A DIARY

1. Try to write in your diary regularly, even if it is not every day.

2. Find a quiet place where you won't be disturbed while writing.

3. Write the date, time, and place at the beginning of each entry.

4. Keep mementos such as photos, movie tickets, and party invitations in your diary.

5. Be as honest as you can about your thoughts and feelings.

6. Find a good hiding place for your diary. You could disguise it by covering it with a dust jacket belonging to a boring book and putting it on your bookshelf.

7. If you're still worried about someone finding it, write a few dull entries in a decoy diary and leave it somewhere obvious.

FAST FLIERS

Peregrine falcon	168 mph (270 kph)
Spine-tailed swift	106 mph (171 kph)
Frigate bird	95 mph (153 kph)
Spur-winged goose	88 mph (142 kph)
Red-breasted merganser	80 mph (129 kph)

REAL-LIFE SUPERHEROES

STRETCHY MAN

British man Gary Turner can stretch his skin to a length of 6.2 in (15.8 cm). By pulling the skin of his neck up and the skin of his forehead down, he can completely cover his face. On November 27, 2004, he clipped 159 wooden clothespins to his face, earning himself a world record.

MR. EAT EVERYTHING

In 1959, Michel Lotito of France developed a taste for metal and glass. So far, he has eaten 18 bicycles, 15 shopping carts, 7 TV sets, 2 beds, 1 pair of skis, and 1 Cessna light aircraft.

THE HUMAN LIGHTNING CONDUCTOR

Roy C. Sullivan of the United States has been struck by lightning no fewer than seven times. He has survived each strike but suffered the following injuries:

1942—lost a big-toe nail

1969—lost both eyebrows

1970—left shoulder burned

1972—hair caught fire

1973—legs burned, hair singed

1976—ankle hurt

1977—stomach and chest burned

COUNTRIES WHOSE NAMES BEGIN AND END WITH THE SAME LETTER

Albania	Australia
Algeria	Austria
Andorra	Czech Republic
Angola	St. Kitts and Nevis
Antigua and Barbuda	St. Vincent and the Grenadines
Argentina	Seychelles
Armenia	Solomon Islands

─────THE THREE-CARD MONTE SCAM─────

1. The scammer shows three playing cards to the audience. One of the cards is a queen.

2. The three cards are placed facedown on a table.

3. The scammer moves the cards around, changing their positions, then invites the audience to place bets on which one is the queen.

4. If the audience members are skeptical and hang back, an accomplice places a bet and wins.

5. Encouraged by this, the audience starts placing bets.

6. The scammer secretly swaps the queen for a different card to ensure that the members of the audience always lose.

7. To keep the bets coming in, every so often the scammer secretly reintroduces the queen and lets someone win. If the scammer is a successful con artist, no audience members will realize they are being conned.

─────────────BIRDCALLS─────────────

Tawny owl..."Hoo hoo-hooo hoo-o-o"

Peregrine falcon......."Haak-haak-haak kee-keee-eeee wheee-ip"

Wren.."Chit chiti tzerr"

Blue tit..."Tsee-tsee-tsee-tsisisisisisi"

Nuthatch.."Pew pew pew chwee chwee"

Bittern.."Boom ker-whoomp"

Middle-spotted woodpecker......."Kvek-kvek-kvek kuk-uk kuk-uk"

Brent goose............................."Kurr-onk kurr-onk kurr-onk"

Laughing gull............................."Hah-hah-hah hoo-hoo hah-hah-hah"

Wood pigeon..................."Coo-ooo-coo-cu-ooo coo-coo-cu-coo"

Egyptian vulture...Silent

————————TEN RULES OF DUELING————————

1. You may use a duel to restore honor if someone has offended you.

2. Challenges are never delivered at night.

3. The duel must take place within a month of the challenge being delivered.

4. The challenged has the right to choose the weapon and the location of the duel.

5. Each combatant nominates a *second* of equal rank in society. The second acts as a go-between—first attempting reconciliation between the parties and then, if this fails, fixing the time and terms of the duel.

6. The duelists start at an agreed distance from each other, armed with swords or pistols.

7. Seconds must reattempt reconciliation after the specified time or number of shots or blows.

8. In the case of pistols, a misfire is counted as a shot.

9. If seconds disagree on anything, they may themselves duel. They should position themselves at right-angles to the challengers to form a cross.

10. Any wound that causes the hand to shake ends the duel.

FUN DUELING WEAPONS

Bananas
Water guns
Flour bombs
Snowballs
Lightsabers
Custard pies
Paper airplanes

---BUBBLE GUM---

The first bubble gum was developed in 1906 by Frank Fleer.
It was named Blibber-Blubber.

In 1928, the bubble gum recipe was improved by an employee
of Frank Fleer named Walter Diemer, resulting in the first widely
sold bubble gum, Dubble Bubble. Diemer colored his creation
pink because it was the only food coloring he had.

Today, over 100,000 tons of bubble gum are chewed every year.

HOW TO BLOW A BUBBLE-GUM BUBBLE

1. Put a big piece of bubble gum in your mouth.

2. Chew it until it's thin and stretchy.

3. Use your tongue to flatten the
gum across the backs of your
top and bottom front teeth.

4. Push the middle of the gum
out between your teeth while
forming a seal all the way
around the gum with your lips.

5. Blow into the stretched gum.

TIPS FOR REMOVING GUM FROM HAIR AND CLOTHING

1. Rub the gum with an ice cube. This will harden the gum,
making it easier to pick and scratch off.

2. Squeeze lemon juice on the gum. This will help reduce
its stickiness.

3. Put a few drops of cooking oil or peanut butter on a
toothbrush and scrub the gum.

> The advertising slogan "Pepsi gives you life"
> was mistranslated into Chinese to "Pepsi
> brings your ancestors back from the grave."

———PLACES TO HIDE A SECRET MESSAGE———

Under a loose floorboard • In the notch of a tree
Under your mattress • On the ledge inside a chimney
Behind a picture frame • In a watertight jar in a pond

———————CAR-TRIP GAMES———————

I SPY
Look around and choose an object for the other passengers
to guess. Let them know the letter the object begins with by
saying "I spy with my little eye something beginning with . . ."
The first person to guess correctly takes the next turn.

ROCK, PAPER, SCISSORS
Hold your right hand in a fist and get a friend to do the same.
Count to three out loud and then, at the same time, each use
your hand to mime either a rock (a fist), a piece of paper (a
flat hand), or a pair of scissors (first two fingers held open).
Rock beats (blunts) scissors. Paper beats (covers) rock.
Scissors beat (cut) paper.

THE ALPHABET GAME
Choose a category such as "things that smell bad," "wild
animals," or "famous people," and think of an example to fit
the chosen category for each letter of the alphabet.

FIRST TO 20
Each choose something to count: for example, yellow cars,
semis from Oklahoma, or squashed animals. The first to count
20 of their chosen category wins.

SING THE MILEAGE SONG
Substitute for X the number of miles you have left to drive
in the following song: "X more miles to go, X more miles
of sorrow, X more miles in this old car, and we'll
be there tomorrow."

APOLOGIZE PROFUSELY FOR SINGING THE MILEAGE SONG
Say "sorry" over and over until you reach your destination.

───────EXTREME CHALLENGES───────

THE POLAR CHALLENGE
368-mile (592-km) trek
to the North Pole.
X-factor: Freezing conditions.

DAKAR MOTOR RALLY
5,600-mile (9,000-km) motor
race across North Africa.
X-factor: The Sahara.

VENDÉE GLOBE
23,000-mile (37,000-km)
nonstop solo sail
around the world.
X-factor: Storms.

DEATH VALLEY
ULTRA-MARATHON
135-mile (217-km) run across
America's Wild West.
X-factor: Soaring
temperatures.

TEXAS WATER SAFARI
Three-day, 262-mile (421-
km) nonstop canoe race
along the Colorado River
to the Gulf of Mexico.
X-factor: Swirling currents.

WESTERN STATES
TRAIL RIDE
100-mile (161-km) 24-hour
horse race across the
Sierra Nevada.
X-factor: Saddle sores.

LA RUTA DE LOS
CONQUISTADORES
300-mile (483-km)
three-day mountain-bike
race in the Costa
Rican jungle.
X-factor: Two volcanoes.

───────SEAFARING SUPERSTITIONS───────

GOOD LUCK

Seeing a black cat before
setting sail

Placing a silver coin under
the masthead

Seeing a swallow

Dolphins swimming
alongside the ship

The feather of a wren killed
on New Year's Day

BAD LUCK

Crossing paths with a
redhead before setting sail

Looking back to port once
you have set sail

Setting sail on a Friday

Killing an albatross

Hearing church bells

Saying the word "drowned"

Drowning

—————————AVIATION LIGHT SIGNALS—————————

If radio communication breaks down, air traffic control uses a light gun to signal messages to the aircraft.

Steady green...Cleared to land

Flashing green...Cleared to approach airport

Steady red.....................Continue circling, give way to other aircraft

Flashing red..Airport unsafe, do not land

Alternating red and green...............................Danger, continue current action with caution

> The word *television* comes from the Greek *tele* for "far" and Latin *visio* for "sight."

—————————IS THIS GO-CART MOVING?—————————

Stare at the wheels of the go-cart below. Jiggle the book and see if you can make the wheels turn.

WHO'S WHO IN A FILM CREW

Producer..In charge of raising money

Director..............Responsible for content of film and performances

Screenwriter...Writes the screenplay

Location manager.....................................Finds the right places to film

Grip..In charge of lighting and rigging

Dolly grip................In charge of moving cameras on the dolly track

Gaffer...Head of the electrical department

Visual effects supervisor...................................Creates special effects

Foley artist....................................Creates and records sound effects

Best boy...Technical assistant

Swing gang...........Team that makes last-minute changes to the set

ALMOST SURELY

In probability theory, the phrase *almost surely* has a precise meaning. It is an event that has zero probability of *not* occurring—i.e., it is *almost surely* going to happen, even though it is still possible that it might not occur.

————————ACCIDENTALLY TASTY————————

CHOCOLATE CHIP COOKIES
In the 1930s, Ruth Wakefield, the owner of the Toll House Inn in Massachusetts, sprinkled chocolate bits into her cookie dough expecting them to melt in the oven. But the chocolate bits held their shape, and instead of making chocolate cookies, she got butter cookies full of chocolate chips.

CORNFLAKES
While working in a hospital in Michigan in 1884, the Kellogg brothers left a pot of wheat-flour mixture out too long. Wondering what would happen, they put the stale wheat through the rollers anyway. Instead of the usual long sheet of dough, they got flakes of wheat that they roasted and served to their patients. They were soon selling their tasty invention under the name Granose.

CRÈME BRÛLÉE
Far from being a traditional French dish, crème brûlée, or "burnt cream," originated, it is said, in 17th-century England. Having accidentally scorched a bowl of custard sprinkled with sugar, the chef at Trinity College, part of Cambridge University, served up the caramelized offering as a new dish. At the university it is still known as "Trinity College cream."

————————FUNKY FESTIVALS————————

THE GREAT TEXAS MOSQUITO FESTIVAL, Clute, TX
Enter your scrawny limbs in the Mosquito-Legs Contest or your best buzz in the Mosquito-Calling Contest.

GILROY GARLIC FESTIVAL, Gilroy, CA
Enter the Smelly King or Queen contest, sample garlic ice cream, and swig garlic drinks.

FROG FESTIVAL, Rayne, LA
Gobble fried frog-legs. Bring your own frog or rent one for the frog-jumping contest.

─────────────THE RICHTER SCALE─────────────

In 1935, U.S. seismologist (earthquake expert) Charles Richter developed a scale for measuring the strength of earthquakes, based on the magnitude of vibrations in the ground. Each level on the scale is ten times greater than the preceding one.

0 to 2....................................Detected by instruments, but not humans

3 to 4...Hanging lights sway and windows rattle

5..............At epicenter, objects fall off shelves and windows shatter

6................Within 6 miles (10 km), chimneys crack and roof tiles fall

7..........Within 60 miles (100 km), the ground cracks and pipes burst

8............................Within 185 miles (300 km), buildings are destroyed

9..Within 620 miles (1,000 km), waves ripple
the ground and buildings and bridges fall

─────────────VIKING NAMES─────────────

Bjorn Ironside • Eric Bloodaxe
Ivar the Boneless • Orvar-Odd
Harold Bluetooth • Sigrid the Haughty
Sigurd Snake-Eye • Halfdan the Black
Hrolf the Walker • Ingvar the Far-Travelled

To work out your own Viking name, either:

Follow your first name with the word "blood-" and the name of your favorite weapon. For example, if your name is Daniel and your favorite weapon is your superstrong thumb, your Viking name would be Daniel Bloodthumb.

or:

Follow your first name with the word "the" and then your most memorable quality—the more evil the better. For example, if your name is James and you are famous for your deadly erupting farts, your Viking name would be James the Eruptor.

26

HOW TO PLAY POOHSTICKS

First of all, you need to find a footbridge spanning running water. Gather your friends together at your chosen spot and tell them to find a stick each. Make sure you can tell the sticks apart. How about attaching a different colored ribbon to each one?

Line everyone up in a row on the bridge, so that the current is flowing toward them and underneath the bridge. Instruct each person to drop their stick on the count of three. When the sticks hit the water, rush over to the other side of the bridge to see whose stick emerges first.

A good tip when playing Poohsticks is to examine the stream or river before the competition. If possible, make sure you are in a position on the bridge to drop your stick into the area of the river where the current is flowing fastest and where the stick will avoid any obstacles, such as rocks or reeds.

MAGIC WORDS

Abracadabra • Hocus-pocus • Open sesame
Izzy-wizzy let's get busy • Ala-kazham

SPY SPEAK

What you say: "It is raining in St. Petersburg."
What you mean: "The teacher is listening."

What you say: "The geese are heading north for the winter."
What you mean: "Meet me in the usual place after school."

What you say: "The roses are beautiful in Moscow this spring."
What you mean: "This is the person I have a crush on."

What you say: "The trains in Berlin always run on time."
What you mean: "Please cover for me."

THE EQUATOR

The equator is an imaginary line that circles Earth halfway between the poles, dividing the planet into a Northern and a Southern Hemisphere. It is about 25,000 miles (40,000 km) long.

There are 13 countries on the equator:

São Tomé and Príncipe • Gabon • Kenya
Republic of Maldives • Indonesia • Kiribati • Ecuador
Democratic Republic of Congo • The Republic of Congo
Uganda • Somalia • Colombia • Brazil

────────HOW TO FIND ORION────────

Orion is one of the largest constellations and was known by the Ancient Greeks as the Great Hunter.

The constellation is home to the famous Orion Nebula, which is a collection of gas and dust which can be seen with the naked eye. You can see Orion wherever you are in the world.

The easiest way to find Orion is to look for the "belt." If you are in the Northern Hemisphere, look to the south and try to pick out three stars in a short, straight line.

If you imagine the constellation as the figure of a hunter, the Orion Nebula is the "sword" that hangs from the belt you have located. To the lower left of the belt is the brightest star in the sky, known as the Dog Star, or Sirius. Betelgeuse is the name of the orange-red star that appears above the belt and to the left.

────────BODILY FLUIDS────────

Pus is made of dead bacteria and dead blood cells.

Boogers are made mostly of sugars; that is why they taste so nice.

You have 250,000 pores on your feet, which produce a quarter of a cup of sweat every day.

You spray about 300 droplets of spit a minute when you are talking.

──CAT WORDS──	──RAT WORDS──
Catalog	Ratatouille
Catapult	Rat-fink
Category	Rattle
Catastrophe	Rat-a-tat
Catamaran	Ratify

POPCORN

Every kernel of popcorn contains a tiny amount of water.
When a kernel is heated, this water turns to steam.
The pressure grows until . . . pop!—the kernel explodes
with a rush of steam. The kernel turns inside out and the
inside expands like white foam.

The first popcorn was made by Native Americans and
flavored with herbs and spices.

The average popping temperature for popcorn
is 347°F (175°C).

A water content of 13.5 percent produces the ideal pop.

Popcorn has been served in movie theaters since 1912.

The average American consumes about 11 gallons (51 liters, or
about 22 microwave popcorn bags) of popcorn every year.

Kernels that fail to pop are known as "old maids."

POPCORN FLAVORS

Salt • Sugar • Caramel • Toffee • Curry

Cherry • Chili • Cinnamon • Double-chocolate

Coconut • Hot mustard • Nacho cheese

HALLOWEEN

Hallows means "holy days" or, in this case, "holy people" or
"saints."
Eve, even, and *e'en* mean "evening" or "night."

In the old Celtic calendar, the year began on November 1, so
the last evening of October was New Year's Eve. Christian
traditions transformed the celebration into All Hallows' Eve or
Hallows' E'en. (All Hallows' Day, November 1, is a day devoted
to the celebration of all the Christian saints.) *Hallows' E'en*
eventually became *Halloween*.

——HOW TO TALK LIKE A PIRATE—BEGINNERS——

"Ahoy, shipmates!"
"Hello, everyone."

"Aye!"
"Yes, I agree."

"Aye aye!"
"I'll get right on that!"

"Avast!"
"Stop!"

"Arrr!"
*Grunt used to fill
pauses in conversation.*

——————————— BEE COLONIES ———————————

A honeybee hive contains thousands of bees of three different types: the queen, the workers, and the drones.

THE QUEEN
A specially nurtured female that emerges from the hive and mates with about 20 drones. She spends the next two years of her life laying eggs.

THE WORKERS
Females that develop from fertilized eggs to make the honey, build and guard the hive, tend the eggs, feed the larvae, and raise the next queen. Workers are sterile and cannot reproduce.

THE DRONES
Stingless males bred from unfertilized eggs purely to mate with the queen. In the process of mating, their vital organs are ripped out and they die. Any drones that don't die in this way are massacred by the workers or kicked out of the hive to starve or die of cold.

COUNTY-FAIR SPORTS

WATERMELON-SEED SPITTING
Contestants eat several pieces of watermelon so that they are left with a pile of watermelon seeds. Players take turns seeing who can spit their seeds the farthest.

"COW PIE" EATING CONTEST
Participants race to see who can eat the most chocolate pie in the shortest amount of time.

FOOT WRESTLING
Two players lie on their backs on a wooden board with the soles of their feet touching. The object is to push the opponent off the board.

GREASY POLE
A greased pole is suspended over water with a flag at the farthest end. Players take turns trying to climb along the pole and reach the flag without falling into the water.

THE ABCs OF LIFESAVING

A is for Airway
Check it is open and not blocked.

B is for Breathing
Make sure it is even and regular.

C is for Circulation
Check for a pulse to make sure blood is circulating around the body.

────── REAL ROCK-STAR REQUESTS ──────

"I want a bowl of M&M's with all the brown ones removed."
"All my food must be wrapped in clear plastic."
"I want the seven dwarves up here now!"
"My coffee always has to be stirred counterclockwise."
"I want my hotel napkins personalized with my initials."
"I want a dimmer switch in my dressing room."
"I want bunny rabbits and kittens backstage
to keep me company."

────────── SLEEPY ANIMALS ──────────

Animal	Hours asleep per day
Koala	22
Little brown bat	19
Python	18
Tiger	15.8
Three-toed sloth	14.4
Cat	12
Human	8
Indian elephant	4
Horse	3
Giraffe	2

──A SONG THAT GETS ON EVERYBODY'S NERVES──

I know a song that gets on everybody's nerves.
I know a song that gets on everybody's nerves.
I know a song that gets on everybody's nerves.
And this is how it goes . . .
[Repeat forever]

———THE WORLD'S COOLEST BUNGEE JUMPS———

CLIFTON SUSPENSION BRIDGE (England)
The Oxford Dangerous Sports Club invented
the modern bungee jump on April 1, 1978. The
first ever bungee jump was from the 249-ft
(76-m) Clifton Suspension Bridge.

BLOUKRANS RIVER BRIDGE (South Africa)
This is the world's highest commercial bungee
jump. Jumpers experience a seven-second
free fall from the 708-ft (216-m) bridge.

THE *GOLDENEYE* DAM
(Switzerland—Italy border)
In the 1995 film *GoldenEye*, James Bond
bungee-jumps over the edge of a dam
in Russia. This dam is in fact on
the Swiss—Italian border, but the
stunt was genuine.

———BORED OF BUNGEE JUMPS? TRY THESE!———

BUNGEE DROP
This is the same as a
bungee jump except that
you cut the cord just
before springing back up
from the ground and
touch down safely.

THE CATAPULT
You start on the ground and
the bungee cord is stretched
from wherever it is fixed.
When released, this pulls
you up into the air at
great speed.

BUNGEE TRAMPOLINE
You are suspended in a
harness from bungee cords
that let you jump much
higher than you normally
could on a trampoline.

BRIDGE SWING
You free-fall from a bridge
and then swing backward
and forward in a long,
high-speed arc (instead of
bouncing up and down
as you would in a
bungee jump).

—— A QUICK GUIDE TO WESTERN PHILOSOPHY——

EXISTENTIALISM
Life has no deeper meaning so I am free to act as I choose. On the other hand, since life has no meaning, I might as well not bother doing anything.

MATERIALISM
Only physical things truly exist. Everything else, such as love or anger or a belief in God, can be explained in physical terms.

FATALISM
Everything that is going to happen is already decided and I have no free will. Since everything will happen the same no matter what I do, I might as well do nothing.

RELATIVISM
There is no right and wrong, and no good and evil. There are only judgments that we agree on.

SOLIPSISM
I am real and so are my experiences, but I can't be sure that anything else exists.

EMPIRICISM
True knowledge comes through practical experience, not thought.

POSTMODERNISM
There is nothing that is true for the whole of humanity. We are therefore free to invent and practice our own philosophies.

——————INUIT WORDS FOR *SNOW*——————

Iñupiaq is a language spoken by Iñupiaq Inuits in Alaska. Here are some of their words for *snow*:

Aniuvak...A mound of packed snow

Apun...Fallen snow

Nutaġaq...Fresh, powdery snow

Piqsiq...Wet snow

Pukak..................Granular snow formed under another layer

Qaŋattaaq...Overhanging snow

Qannik...Falling snow

Silliq...Crusty, hard snow

---LEGALLY BLIND---

A legally blind person has to stand 20 ft (6 m) away from an object to see it with the same degree of clarity as a normally sighted person can from 200 ft (61 m), even when wearing the best glasses.

---TRADITIONAL CAKES---

Pumpkin pie..United States

Moon cake...China

Victoria sponge..England

Poppyseed cake..Poland

Pavlova...New Zealand

Lady fingers...France

Cheesecake..Ancient Greece

Black Forest gâteau...Germany

> Due to the nature of infinity, an infinite number of monkeys randomly hitting the keys of a typewriter will eventually type out the complete works of William Shakespeare.

MISSING TREASURE

THE CROWN JEWELS OF MARIE ANTOINETTE
In 1792, the jewels of the beheaded French queen Marie Antoinette were stolen by revolutionaries. The Sancy Diamond and French Blue Diamond were never recovered.

KING JOHN'S TREASURE
The King of England lost his treasure, including the Crown Jewels, when horses pulling a carriage containing the treasure got disoriented in a swirling fog. They dragged the treasure carriage into a murky stretch of water.

NAZI GOLD
During World War II, Nazis in Germany looted foreigners' treasures. Gold was transferred into top-secret Swiss banks and never heard of again.

THE KNIGHTS' TEMPLAR TREASURE
This powerful order of medieval knights were thought to have been the guardians of the Holy Grail. To this day the Grail's whereabouts allegedly remains a closely guarded secret.

Chinese gooseberries come from New Zealand.

HOW TO TALK LIKE A PIRATE—ADVANCED

"The Sun be over the yardarm, 'tis time for victuals, and smartly, me hearty!"
"It's getting late—hurry up with dinner, I'm starving, mate!"

"Let's see what's crawled out of the bunghole."
"Let's see what's for dinner."

"Bring me a noggin of rum, now, won't you, matey?"
"Can I have a drink?"

"The cat's out of the bag, the wind's gone out of me sails, and I'll be swinging from the yardarm afore eight bells."
"I'm in big trouble."

NOT-SO-SECRET DIARIES

THE SECRET DIARY OF
ADRIAN MOLE, AGE 13³/₄
Written by Sue Townsend,
this diary of Adrian Mole
(there are now six) tells
of an English teenage
boy's growing pains.

THE DIARY
OF SAMUEL PEPYS
This 17th-century Londoner
wrote his diaries in a code
that wasn't cracked until
long after his death. He
wrote about the things he
saw firsthand, including the
Great Fire of London and
public executions.

THE DIARY OF
ANNE FRANK
Anne Frank was a Jewish girl
who went into hiding from the
Nazis in Amsterdam during
World War II. She kept a diary
for the two years that she
spent in a secret annex
of a house.

CAPTAIN SCOTT'S
JOURNAL
Robert Falcon Scott
kept a diary of his team's
expedition to the South
Pole in 1912. He and four
others died shortly after
reaching the pole.

HOW TO BECOME A SAINT

1. Die. In Roman Catholicism, you cannot usually become
   a saint until at least five years after your death.

2. Local bishops must investigate your life and send their
   findings to the Pope.

3. The Pope proclaims you are a virtuous role model.

4. Two miracles must occur because of you.
   (Officially, a miracle must involve no trickery and must
   also suspend the laws of nature.)

The worst Viking vengeance was known as the Blood-
Red Eagle. The enemy's back was cut open, his ribs
were pulled from his spine, and his lungs were removed.

──THE WORLD'S LONGEST STARING CONTEST──

─────────OXYMORONS─────────

Oxymorons are words that are used together that have contradictory meanings. They don't make any sense, but they make complete sense.

Living dead
Seriously funny
Same difference
Virtual reality
Almost exactly
Deafening silence
Clearly confused

─────────SIXTH SENSE─────────

Intuition...A gut feeling about something

Déjà vu.........................The feeling of having seen something before

Telepathy.........The ability to pass thoughts from person to person

Medium.................Someone who can sense the presence of spirits

Visionary....A person who can see into the future through dreams

Mind-reading............................Tuning in to another person's thoughts

NATURAL HAIRSTYLES

Widow's peak....................V-shaped point in middle of the forehead

Cowlick.....................Swirl of unruly hair that can't be combed down

Crown....................................A whorl of hair at the center of the scalp

Double crown............Two whorls of hair at the center of the scalp

HOW FAR CAN YOU SEE?

ON A CLEAR DAY
As far as the Sun, 93 million miles (150 million km) away

ON A CLEAR NIGHT
As far as the Andromeda Galaxy, 2 million light-years away
(one light-year is nearly
6 million million miles [9.5 million million km])

WITH THE BEST TELESCOPE
14 billion light years away

The fastest speed ever reached on a skateboard was 62.5 mph (100.6 kph). The skater was Gary Hardwick of California.

HEALING CRYSTALS

Amethyst...Peace and harmony

Carnelian..Focus

Citrine..Mental clarity

Quartz...Energy and healing

Amber..Digestion and reproduction

Tiger's-eye..Well-being and confidence

Tourmaline...Purity and protection

————————ALLEGED MERPEOPLE SIGHTINGS————

ENGLAND, 1167
A merman was
washed up onto the
beach at Orford,
Suffolk. He was kept
in Orford Castle for
six months before
escaping back
into the sea.

POLAND, 1531
A mermaid caught by fishermen in the Baltic Sea was sent
to the King of Poland. She died after three days in captivity.

CEYLON, 1560
Seven merpeople were sighted by passengers on board
a boat bound for India, off the west coast of Ceylon (now
Sri Lanka). Witnesses included the Viceroy of Goa.

IRELAND, 1819
A young mermaid was caught off the Irish coast. She was the
size of a ten-year-old child, with long hair and dark eyes. A boy
shot at her with a gun and she disappeared back into the sea.

——THE YOSEMITE SYSTEM OF MOUNTAINEERING——

The Yosemite system of mountaineering grades the
difficulty of climbing routes.

Class 1..Hiking

Class 2....................Simple scrambling with occasional use of hands

Class 3................................Scrambling with occasional aid of a rope

Class 4..........Simple climbing with exposure and possible fatal falls

Class 5..Technical free-climbing

Class 6........................Artificial or aid climbing; for example, climbing
a rope up a sheer face with no holds

DO-IT-YOURSELF PEOPLE

GOLEM

In Jewish folklore, a golem was a humanlike creature made of clay and brought to life by a holy man. The golem could not speak and would perform tasks for the holy man. Often he would cause trouble by taking a task too literally.

FRANKENSTEIN'S MONSTER

In Mary Shelley's novel *Frankenstein*, the Swiss scientist Dr. Frankenstein creates a monster out of body parts taken from local graveyards and dissecting rooms. The monster wreaks havoc after he is shunned by the horrified doctor.

HOMUNCULUS

According to the 15th-century Austrian alchemist Paracelsus, a homunculus was a humanlike being made in the warmth of horse manure and nourished by human blood. Marvelous creatures such as pygmies, wood sprites, and giants were all homunculi.

PINOCCHIO

In the children's story by the Italian author Carlo Collodi, a wooden puppet made by the childless carpenter Geppetto comes to life. After proving his worth, the puppet, called Pinocchio, is magically turned into a real boy.

FEATS OF GREAT STRENGTH

Performing one-fingered push-ups
Ripping up a telephone book
Bending a steel bar
Breaking metal chains
Lifting a car
Pushing a bus with your head
Pulling a Boeing 747

THE COLOR OF NOISE

If sound waves are translated into light waves, different sounds appear as different colors.

Sound waves	Light waves
TV static, urban traffic	White
Rushing water or ocean surf	Pink
Subway train, noisy air-conditioning system	Red
Roomful of five-year-olds playing recorders	Orange
Piercing hiss	Blue
Random footsteps	Brown
Natural background noise	Green
Silence	Black

> Identical twins usually die within three years of each other.

UNLIKELY PARTNERSHIPS

THE CLOWN FISH AND THE SEA ANEMONE
The clown fish is immune to the anemone's stinging tentacles. It keeps the anemone's tentacles clean and in return is protected from predators.

THE ANT AND THE CATERPILLAR
Some Australian caterpillars have special glands that produce a honeylike liquid that ants like to drink. In return, the ants protect the defenseless caterpillar from parasites.

THE PILOT FISH AND THE SHARK
Tiny pilot fish swim into sharks' mouths and nibble away any rotting food caught between the sharks' teeth. Sharks rarely eat these swimming toothpicks and instead help them by scaring off would-be predators.

THE KNIGHTS' CODE

Rescue damsels in distress.

Love your country.

Defend your monarch.

Respect your fellow knights.

Never refuse a challenge.

Don't hide from your enemies.

Live honorably and fight for glory.

Give to the poor.

Protect the weak.

Stand up against injustice.

Don't tell lies.

Always finish what you begin.

AMAZING ANIMAL STATS

1. If you attach a magnet to a homing pigeon's neck, it won't be able to find its way home.
2. A giraffe can run faster than a horse and go longer without water than a camel.
3. A snail can sleep for three years.
4. All polar bears are left-handed, so if one is chasing you, stay to the right.
5. Robins eat 3 miles' worth of earthworms in a year.
6. Sheep can survive up to two weeks buried in snowdrifts.
7. Cows and cats both get hairballs.
8. Even bloodhounds can't smell the difference between identical twins.
9. A crocodile cannot chew, but its digestive juices can dissolve steel.

INTERESTING BRIDGES

BRIDGE OF SIGHS, VENICE, ITALY
Prisoners crossed this bridge before being taken to their cells.
It is said they would sigh as they took their last view of Venice.

LONDON BRIDGE, LONDON, ENGLAND
Until 1750, this was the only bridge over the River Thames.
Heads of traitors were placed on spikes above the
southern gate of the bridge.

MILLAU BRIDGE, MASSIF CENTRAL MOUNTAINS, FRANCE
1,125 ft (343 m) tall at its highest point, this bridge is
taller than the Eiffel Tower.

THE FORTH RAIL BRIDGE, QUEENSFERRY, SCOTLAND
This Victorian bridge is so long that, until recent developments
in paint technology, it had to be continuously painted—as
soon as the people painting it had finished, it was time
to start at the beginning again!

GOLDEN GATE BRIDGE, SAN FRANCISCO, USA
When it was built in 1937, this was the largest suspension
bridge in the world. Today, the Akashi Kaikyo Bridge in
Japan holds that title.

MATHEMATICAL BRIDGE, CAMBRIDGE, ENGLAND
It was rumored to have been designed by Sir Isaac Newton
without the use of nuts or bolts to hold the wood together.
According to legend, students dismantled the bridge one
night but were unable to put it back together. It was
then rebuilt using nuts and bolts.

COOL GADGETS (REAL & IMAGINARY)

Bulletproof jacket • Lock-picking kit • Micro-tracers
Grappling hook • Wrist radio • Smoke-screen pellets
Anti-puncture bike tires • Infrared glasses
Anti-gravity hovering skateboard
Superstrong rope contained in a yo-yo

———THE WORLD'S SIMPLEST CARD TRICK———

1. Shuffle the deck in front of a friend.

2. Secretly peek at the card on the bottom and remember it.

3. Ask your friend to pick a card, any card, from the deck and look at it carefully without showing you.

4. Cut the cards—take the top half of the deck in your left hand and the bottom half in your right hand.

5. Hold out the left-hand pile and tell your friend to put his or her card on top of it.

6. Put the cards from your right hand on top of the pile.

7. You can now work through the pack, card by card, until you come to the card originally on the bottom of the pack. Your friend's card is the next one, but go past it so that it looks like you've missed it.

8. Return to the correct card and sit back as your friend stares at you in awe and amazement.

———————HOW LOUD IS A DECIBEL?———————

0 decibels	Threshold of hearing
10	Human breathing
15	Whisper
80	Vacuum cleaner
90	Loud factory (harmful)
120	Rock concert
130	Train horn
150	Rifle firing
170	(eardrums rupture)
180	Blue whale humming
250	Inside a tornado (death to humans)

----------A WARNING TO PIRATES----------

The notorious British pirate Captain Kidd
was hanged at Execution Dock in
London on May 23, 1701. On the
first attempt, the rope broke,
so Kidd was strung up and
hanged again. His body was
suspended in the sea and
left for the tide to wash
over it three times. Then it
was painted in tar, bound in
chains, and hung up in a
metal cage. His rotting
corpse served as a warning
to pirates sailing in and out of
London.

----------SWITCHING ON A LIGHT----------

The speed of light is approximately 186,000 miles per second
(300,000 km per second). If you could slow this down to 1 foot
per second, you would be able to see the way shadows are
gradually chased away when you turn on a light:

You flick the light switch. For a while nothing happens.

After a few seconds, the lightbulb gradually begins to light up,
but the room remains completely dark.

Slowly a sphere of light begins to spread around the
bulb, creating a halo effect. Gradually the sphere of light
expands to fill the room.

The room is now completely illuminated, apart from the
shadows, which remain pitch-black.

Light bouncing off the walls begins to fill the shadows, and
eventually they start to lighten.

You switch off the light. The shadows are the last areas
to return to pitch-black.

HOW TO RIP A PHONE BOOK IN HALF

1. Place the phone book on a tabletop in front of you and open as near to the middle as possible. Holding it as shown above, bend the book by pushing down with your two thumbs.

2. Now grasp the phone book firmly, bending the ends down so that the middle of the book forms a V shape.

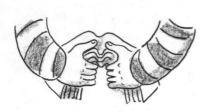

3. Keep pressing the ends down until the pages start to split.

4. Now push one half of the book down while pulling the other half up, until it tears in two.

The world record for ripping up phone books is held by Ed Shelton of the United States. On November 18, 2005, he ripped up 55 phone books from top to bottom in three minutes.

THE GAME

The Game is a mental game. The aim of The Game is to forget that you are playing it. As many players as you want can play. Players need to be aware of only a few simple rules:

1. To know of The Game's existence is to play The Game.
2. To realize you have thought of The Game is to lose The Game.
3. When you lose, you must immediately announce, "I have lost The Game."
4. If anyone present asks "What is The Game?" you must explain these rules.
5. Other players of The Game who are present when you announce that you have lost have a 30-minute grace period in which to forget about The Game before they also lose.
6. It is not possible to know that you have won The Game, only to have won it and remain ignorant of the fact.

THE HIGHEST MOUNTAINS ON MARS

Olympus Mons............................16.8 miles (27 km)

Ascraeus Mons..............................6.8 miles (11 km)

Arsia Mons.....................................5.6 miles (9 km)

Pavonis Mons.................................4.3 miles (7 km)

Alba Patera....................................1.9 miles (3 km)

The highest mountain on Earth is Mount Everest, which is only 5.5 miles (8.85 km) high.

RUSSIAN
SPACE DOGS

Laika • Belka • Strelaka
Chernushka • Veterok
Ugolyok

AMERICAN
SPACE MONKEYS

Albert • Gordo • Able
Baker • Sam • Bonny
Scatback

──SUPERHEROES YOU PROBABLY DON'T KNOW──

ULTRAMAN (Japan)
132-foot (40-m) tall alien from
Nebula M78. He can fly
at seven times the speed
of sound and can spend only
three minutes on
Earth at a time.

MONKEY KING (China)
Born out of a rock, the
Monkey King is very strong
and extraordinarily clever. He
uses a magic staff he got from
the Dragon Kings of the
Oceans as his favorite
weapon—it can expand or
shrink at its owner's command.

EL BULBO (Mexico)
Brought to life when a
spell was cast on the
bulbs in a television set, El
Bulbo is a superhero who
fights his archrival and fellow
lightbulb Adolfo.
He can fly, grow to an
enormous size, and
fire destructive rays.

NAGRAJ (India)
Microscopic snakes living in
his bloodstream give him
superhuman strength, a
venomous bite, and snakes
that shoot out of his wrists.

> Scientists think it likely that the universe
> was created 13.7 billion years ago.

────REVOLUTIONS────

AMERICAN REVOLUTION
The 13 colonies of America broke away from Great Britain
and became a republic of united states, 1775–83.

FRENCH REVOLUTION
Overthrow of the French monarchy and aristocracy and the
establishment of a French republic, 1789–99.

RUSSIAN REVOLUTION
Abdication of Czar Nicholas II and the establishment
of the Soviet Union, 1917.

VELVET REVOLUTION
Bloodless overthrow of Communist government in
Czechoslovakia, 1989.

FENCING TERMS

A bout..A fencing match

Salute.............A courteous gesture at the start and finish of a bout

Allee!...The command to begin

Parry...A defensive stroke

Riposte...A counterattack after a parry

Esquive...............................Ducking or sidestepping to avoid being hit

Pattinando...A lunge

Coulé..A glide

Prise de fer..Taking the opponent's blade

Finale...........................The last move in a series of attacking actions

PANGRAMS

Pangrams are sentences that contain every letter of
the alphabet at least once.

The quick brown fox jumps over the lazy dog.

The five boxing wizards jump quickly.

Five or six jet planes zoomed quickly by the tower.

──────────── FREE-RUNNING MOVES ────────────

Free running is usually practiced in urban areas and is a way of moving through the environment fluidly. Free runners use a series of vaults, jumps, and athletic movements to pass through, over, and under everyday obstacles such as stairs, railings, and walls.

Wall climb..Scaling a vertical surface

Underbar..Jumping or swinging through a gap

Gap jump...................................Jumping from one location to another

Turn vault.................................Vaulting to the other side of an object

Tic-tac...............................Kicking off one surface to clear another

Rail precision..............................Jumping from one railing to another

Cat balance................................Running on hands and feet along a
railing or narrow surface

──────── THE FIVE KINGDOMS OF LIVING THINGS ────────

Monerans   Organisms with simple cell structures; for
example, bacteria.

Protists   Simple organisms with nuclei and other complex
cell structures; for example, some algae.

Fungi   Primitive plants that decompose dead plant and
animal matter; for example, mushrooms and yeast.

Plants   Multicellular organisms, usually with cell walls
composed mainly of cellulose. Plants typically
use sunlight as an energy source and convert
light energy, water, and carbon dioxide into
glucose, oxygen, and water through a process
called photosynthesis.

Animals   Multicellular organisms that feed on other
organisms. Almost all animals can respond to
changes in their environment by moving all or
part of their bodies.

---A KNIGHTLY TOURNAMENT---

JOUST

Knights on horseback charge at each other with long lances under their arms. The aim is to knock your opponent off his horse.

MELÉE À PIED

Knights fight on foot with blunted swords. You win if you strike your opponent three times.

ARCHERY

Knights shoot 12 arrows at the center of a target, scoring points for accuracy. The best shot wins.

WRESTLING

Knights fight unarmed and the winner is decided by the best of five throws.

---REALLY STUPID---

A woman in Texas had bought a new car and wanted to check out the size of the trunk. She asked her family members to shut her inside it, then realized she was still holding the keys.

While out hunting in Arizona, a man accidentally shot himself in the leg. To try to attract the attention of someone who could rescue him, he fired his gun a second time. Unfortunately, he shot himself in the other leg.

A shopkeeper in Texas accepted a fake $100 bill, even though it was over a foot long.

Some British soldiers, who were standing in for fire-rescue services during a strike in 1978, were called to help an old lady rescue her cat from a tree. Mission accomplished, she invited them in for some tea and cookies. Afterward, the soldiers waved good-bye, got in their vehicle, and ran over the cat.

TRACKING FOOTPRINTS

Grizzly bear

Duck

Beaver

Wild pig

Hedgehog

Monster

WAVE-HEIGHT SCALE

Glassy...0 ft (0 m)

Rippled...1 to 2 ft (0.3 to 0.6 m)

Choppy...2 to 4 ft (0.6 to 1.2 m)

Very rough...13 to 20 ft (4 to 6 m)

Mid-ocean storm waves...................................20 to 30 ft (6 to 9 m)

Extreme waves...50 to 100 ft (15 m to 30 m)

Freak waves..100 ft+ (30 m+)

——THE WORLD'S MOST DANGEROUS ANIMALS——

POLAR BEAR
Found only in the Arctic, the polar bear is the largest land carnivore and is twice the size of a tiger. It hunts both on land and in the sea, camouflaged white against the snow. When food is scarce, polar bears may kill and eat humans.

GREAT WHITE SHARK
Up to 20 feet (6 m) long and weighing over 4,400 pounds (2,000 kg), the great white shark is the world's largest predatory fish. Great whites ambush their prey by swimming up from the bottom of the sea. They have extra rows of teeth behind their main ones that are constantly growing. Their teeth are retractable, like a cat's claws.

BOX JELLYFISH
Also known as the sea wasp, this cube-shaped jellyfish is found only in tropical seas. Its tentacles unleash fast-working venom that can shut down a human victim's heart and lungs in as little as three minutes. It kills more people every year than any other sea creature.

FUNNEL-WEB SPIDER
The world's deadliest spider comes from Australia, where it likes to live in cool, sheltered habitats. The males are known to bite aggressively and repeatedly. Death can occur any time from 15 minutes to 3 days after the bite.

INLAND TAIPAN SNAKE
Found in Central Australia, this snake has 0.5-inch (12-mm) long fangs. It has the most lethal venom in the world, and one bite contains enough poison to kill several adult humans.

KOMODO DRAGON
The largest lizard in the world, the Komodo dragon hunts live prey on the island of Komodo in Indonesia. Deadly bacteria in the dragon's mouth quickly kill a bitten victim.

KILLER BEES
These extremely aggressive bees have a tendency to swarm. They have a high proportion of soldier bees that guard their hive and pursue and sting perceived threats over long distances.

────────────────REAL CRAYON COLORS────────────────

Magenta	Tan	Sea green
Pink sherbert	Wheat	Aquamarine
Crimson	Moccasin	Turquoise
Tomato	Almond	Cyan
Coral	Khaki	Teal
Salmon	Dandelion	Azure
Indian red	Lemon yellow	Sky blue
Fire brick	Gold	Navy
Maroon	Spring green	Midnight blue
Chocolate	Lawn green	Slate blue
Sienna	Lime	Cornflower blue
Sunset orange	Olive	Royal blue
Apricot	Forest	Steel blue
Goldenrod	Jungle green	Orchid

───────────TECTONIC───────────
PLATES

Earth's crust is made up of slabs
of rock, known as tectonic plates,
that are in constant motion.

African Plate	Juan de Fuca Plate
Antarctic Plate	Nazca Plate
Arabian Plate	North American Plate
Australian Plate	Pacific Plate
Caribbean Plate	Philippine Plate
Cocos Plate	Scotia Plate
Eurasian Plate	South American Plate
Indian Plate	

──SERVING──
PLATES

Plates from which
food is served
or eaten.

Dinner plate
Saucer
Side plate
Platter
Spinning plate
Trencher
Paper plate
Ashet

—THE OFFICIAL ROUTE TO DRACULA'S CASTLE—

Day One: Catch the 8:35 P.M. overnight train from Munich in Bavaria to the Austrian capital, Vienna, arriving at 6:46 A.M.

Day Two: After breakfasting in Vienna, take the early train to the Hungarian capital, Budapest. There, catch a connecting train, arriving at nightfall in the Transylvanian town of Klausenburgh, also known as Cluj-Napoca. Stay the night at the Hotel Royale.

Day Three: Take the 7:55 A.M. train to the northern Transylvanian city of Bistritz, also known as Bistrita. Arrive at dusk and stay at the Golden Krone Hotel, recommended by Count Dracula.

Day Four: Accept the crucifix given to you by the fearful hotelier when he discovers you are traveling to Dracula's Castle. Take the early-morning stagecoach to Bukovinia, on the northeastern slopes of the Carpathian Mountains of Transylvania.

Day Five: At precisely midnight, you will be dropped on the Borgo Pass, a lonely road that runs into the heart of the mountains. After a terrifying wait in the dark, a horseman will meet you and take you through a wolf-infested forest and blizzarding snow to Castle Dracula.

———ANIMALS THAT GIVE BIRTH TO CALVES———

Buffalo • Elephants • Cows • Giraffes • Hippopotamuses
Moose • Camels • Antelope • Elks • Whales • Dolphins

──────────── FAMOUS EQUATIONS ────────────

THE DEFINITION OF PI

Pi (π) is the ratio of the length of a circle's outer edge (circumference) to the distance across its center (diameter). It is always the same, regardless of the size of the circle, and is roughly equal to 3.141592653.

$$\pi = \frac{c}{d}$$

π = pi
c = circumference of the circle
d = diameter of the circle

EINSTEIN'S THEORY OF RELATIVITY

Albert Einstein discovered that when an object has mass, it has an amount of energy related to that mass. The following equation works on the principle that the resting energy of an object is equal to its mass multiplied by the square of the speed of light:

$$E = mc^2$$

E = energy
m = mass
c = the speed of light

NEWTON'S GRAVITY LAW

Every object that has mass (weight) also has a gravitational pull. The larger the object, the stronger the pull. Every object, therefore, attracts every other object with a gravitational force that is proportional to each of their masses and the distance between them:

$$F = \frac{Gm_1m_2}{d^2}$$

F = force of gravitational attraction between two masses (m_1 and m_2)
G = gravitational constant (the force of gravity that is constantly present)
d = distance between the two masses

PYTHAGORAS'S THEOREM

In a right-angled triangle, the sum of the squares of the two shortest sides is equal to the square of the longest side:

$$a^2 + b^2 = c^2$$

a = short side of a right-angled triangle
b = other short side of a right-angled triangle
c = long side of a right-angled triangle

──TIGHTROPE FEATS OF THE GREAT BLONDIN──

The Great Blondin was the greatest daredevil ever to cross Niagara Falls. On June 30, 1859, he walked on a tightrope over the falls. When he got to the center he lowered a rope to a boat below, pulled up a bottle, and sat down on his tightrope for a drink. He went on to perform the following amazing feats over the huge waterfall:

cooking an omelet

riding a bicycle

doing a backward somersault

walking with his hands and feet tied

walking blindfolded

pushing a wheelbarrow

carrying his manager on his back

──────HOW FAST IS STANDING STILL?──────

Earth is spinning around the Sun at approximately 70,000 mph (112,000 kph). Meanwhile, the solar system is traveling through space at 170 miles per second (273 km per second).

──HOW MANY TO CHANGE A LIGHTBULB?──

Owls...................................None. Owls aren't afraid of the dark.

Martians...One and a half.

Monkeys........................Three. One to change the lightbulb and two to throw bananas at each other.

Poltergeists............................Two. One to hold the lightbulb and the other to twist the room around.

---PERFORMANCE ART YOU CAN DO---

Do five push-ups and have a friend count really loudly:
"996, 997, 998, 999, 1,000!"

Juggle uncooked eggs but keep dropping them.

Follow passersby and impersonate the way they walk.

Sing out of tune through a traffic cone.

Talk to an imaginary person trapped down a grate.

Stand on a box and clear your throat as if you are about
to sing. Then clear your throat some more, and just
keep on clearing your throat.

Pretend you have jelly legs and keep wobbling and falling
over and getting up and falling over again.

Draw ugly portraits of passersby.

---BAD LUCK AT THE THEATER---

Whistling or clapping backstage.

Saying "*Macbeth*." (Instead, say "The Scottish play.")

Wishing someone good luck. (Instead, say "Break a leg.")

Turning off the light when the stage is not in use.

——MAGICAL BEASTS IN HARRY POTTER NOVELS——

HIPPOGRIFF
Beast of the air and of the ground, it has the head, forelegs, and wings of a giant eagle and the body of a horse.
A stickler for the formalities of good manners, the hippogriff will be irritable if bows are not exchanged by way of greeting.

CENTAUR
Intelligent being with the head and torso of a human and the body of a horse. Equally mistrustful of Muggles and wizards, centaurs live deep in forests.

HUNGARIAN HORNTAIL
Scaly black dragon with yellow eyes. Frequent jets of flame are fired from its jaws, and a blow from its spiked tail can be deadly.

WEREWOLF
When the moon is full, this otherwise perfectly reasonable human turns into a bloodthirsty beast. The curse is caught from the bite of another werewolf, and there is no known cure. Werewolves are to be pitied, but not at close range on the night of a full moon.

DOXY
Tiny, winged creature with four legs, four arms, and a thick covering of black fur. They have venomous teeth and a deadly bite.

BASILISK
Venomous-fanged serpent with a deadly stare. Illegally produced by hatching a chicken's egg under a toad.

——THE THREE OFFICIAL TYPES OF FREAK WAVE——

WALL OF WATER
A wave that is preceded by a deep trough, known as a "hole in the sea," and travels up to 6 miles (10 km) through the ocean.

THREE SISTERS
Groups of three huge waves.

GIANT STORM WAVE
A single wave that grows to up to four times the normal height of a storm wave, then collapses after a few seconds.

ANIMAL DEFENSES

BADGERS
The skin on a badger's bottom is so baggy that if a predator gets its teeth into it, the badger is able to twist around and bite back.

RABBITS
A rabbit's eyes are set on the sides of its head. This increases the rabbit's field of vision and allows it to keep watch for predators, even while eating.

IO MOTHS
When threatened, these moths pull back their upper wings to reveal markings like a pair of eyes. This startles the attacker and gives the moth time to escape.

PUFFER FISH
These unusual fish can inflate themselves to several times their normal size by swallowing water or air.

HEDGEHOGS
When threatened by predators, hedgehogs roll up into a ball of prickles.

SKUNKS
Skunks spray a sticky and foul-smelling fluid at predators. The stench is strong enough to put off even the hardiest bear.

HOMONYMS

Homonyms are words that sound the same but are spelled differently and have different meanings.

Karat–Carrot
Ate–Eight
Knead–Need
Wait–Weight
Dear–Deer
Knight–Night

Plain–Plane
Some–Sum
For–Four
You–Ewe
Pail–Pale
Scent–Cent

EVERYDAY CONUNDRUMS

CATCH-22

Sometimes called a vicious circle, a catch-22 is a situation in which you have to do one thing to achieve another, but you can't achieve the first thing until you've achieved the second:

"I can't make money from washing cars until I've bought the equipment I need, but I can't buy the equipment I need until I've made some money from washing cars."

MORTON'S FORK

A choice between two equally unpleasant alternatives:

"You can do your homework first and then clean your bedroom, or you can clean your bedroom first and then do your homework."

HOBSON'S CHOICE

An apparently free choice that is really no choice at all:

"You can have either of these two chocolates, as long as I can have that one."

FAMOUS NUMBERS

007..James Bond

666...The number of the Beast

2000...The second millennium, or Y2K

9/11.............The date of the terrorist attacks on New York in 2001

180...........................The highest possible score in the game of darts

13...Unlucky number

365...Days in a year (except leap years)

186,292..................................The speed of light in miles per second

9¾...............................The train platform from which the Hogwarts Express departs in the Harry Potter books

80............The number of days it takes to go around the world in Jules Verne's novel *Around the World in Eighty Days*

ASSASSINATED LEADERS

MOHANDAS K. GANDHI
A pacifist campaigner for Indian independence, Gandhi was shot three times by his enemy Nathuram Godse on January 30, 1948.

ARCHDUKE FRANZ FERDINAND
Franz Ferdinand was the heir to the throne of Austria-Hungary. His assassination by Gavrilo Princip on June 28, 1914, sparked World War I.

ABRAHAM LINCOLN
This president of the United States was assassinated on April 14, 1865, while watching a theater performance. The assassin was John Wilkes Booth, who shot the president in the back of the head.

JOHN FITZGERALD KENNEDY
When this president of the United States was shot in the head on November 22, 1963, a man named Lee Harvey Oswald was accused. Many people believe that Oswald was either framed or part of a larger conspiracy.

GAIUS JULIUS CAESAR
On March 15, 44 B.C., the Roman emperor Julius Caesar was stabbed 23 times while he slept in his bed. The assassination was carried out by a conspiracy of Roman senators, one of whom was Caesar's friend Brutus.

THE MINERAL-HARDNESS SCALE

The Mohs' scale is a system for classifying mineral hardness. Each mineral can make a scratch in those below it in the scale.

10. Diamond (hardest)
9. Corundum
8. Topaz
7. Quartz
6. Orthoclase
5. Apatite
4. Fluorite
3. Calcite
2. Gypsum
1. Talc (softest)

────────HOW TO READ TEA LEAVES────────

Drink a cup of loose leaf tea from a plain white cup and leave a small amount of liquid in the bottom. Hold the cup in your left hand and swirl the liquid around three times in a clockwise direction, making sure that the leaves reach the rim but don't spill over. Turn the cup upside down

onto a saucer, letting the liquid drain away. After seven seconds, turn the cup back the right-way up and hold it so that the handle points toward you. You can use the patterns created to predict the future:

Acorn	Success will be yours
Bell	You will receive unexpected news
Cat	A friend will lie
Dagger	Beware of danger
Face	You will make a new friend
Goat	Beware of enemies
Harp	You will fall in love
Rabbit	You will need to be brave
Ship	You will go on a long journey
Tree	Good health will be yours
Wheel	You will get good exam results
Zebra	There will be a dramatic change in your life

───────────────BIKES───────────────

Quadracycle • Penny farthing • Unicycle • Tandem
Exercise bike • Racing bike • Mountain bike • BMX

————THE OFFICIAL RULES OF THE "WORLD———— CHERRY-PIT-SPIT CHAMPIONSHIP"

1. Each cherry is put in the mouth whole and the flesh eaten before spitting the pit. The pit is the stone in the middle of the cherry.

2. The longest of three spits is recorded. If a pit is swallowed, that spit is forfeited.

3. No foreign objects may be held in the mouth that might give an advantage in spitting the pit.

4. No popping the cheeks. The spitter's hands must remain below the shoulders.

5. Contestants' feet may not touch or cross the foul line.

   The longest recorded spit is 93 ft, 6.5 in (28.5 m).

An anaconda snake can eat a 6-foot, 7-inch (2-m) long crocodile.

————————————CULTURAL SYMBOLS————————

COUNTRY	ANIMAL(S)	FOOD
Germany	Black eagle	Sauerkraut
United States	Bald eagle, bison	Hamburger
England	Lion, bulldog	Fish and chips
Wales	Red dragon	Laver bread
Australia	Kangaroo	Barbecue
France	Rooster	Frogs' legs
Scotland	Red lion	Haggis
Spain	Bull	Paella, tapas
Russia	Eagle, bear	Borscht
Canada	Beaver	Maple syrup

THE STORY OF WEAPONS

2,500,000 B.C...Stone tools first used

6,000 B.C..Metal spears first thrown

2,000 B.C.......................Celtic tribes fight using horse-drawn chariots

400 B.C.................Ancient Greeks use ballistae (giant bolt-throwers)

A.D. 950...Chinese invent gunpowder

1128..Chinese first use cannons

1400..Shotguns first used

1914–18...................World War I—tanks first used instead of horses

1939–45.......................................World War II—assault rifles first used

1945............................Allies use the first atomic bombs against Japan

SHOOTING STARS

METEOR
An object falling through the atmosphere—most are
small bits of rock or metal.

METEORITE
A meteor that hits Earth.

METEOROID
An object outside Earth's atmosphere that would become a
meteor if it entered the atmosphere.

FAMOUS BEGINNINGS

"Once there were four children whose names were Peter, Susan, Edmund, and Lucy."

The Lion, the Witch, and the Wardrobe, by C. S. Lewis

"Alice was beginning to get very tired of sitting by her sister on the bank, and of having nothing to do: once or twice she had peeped into the book her sister was reading, but it had no pictures or conversations in it, 'and what is the use of a book,' thought Alice, 'without pictures or conversations?'"

Alice's Adventures in Wonderland, by Lewis Carroll

"Here is Edward Bear, coming downstairs now, bump, bump, bump, on the back of his head, behind Christopher Robin."

Winnie-the-Pooh, by A. A. Milne

"Mr. and Mrs. Dursley, of number four, Privet Drive, were proud to say that they were perfectly normal, thank you very much."

Harry Potter and the Sorcerer's Stone, by J. K. Rowling

"Lyra and her daemon moved through the darkening hall, taking care to keep to one side, out of sight of the kitchen."

The Golden Compass, by Philip Pullman

PAPER SIZES

A0......33.1 × 46.8 in (841 × 1,189 mm)

A1......23.4 × 33.1 in (594 × 841 mm)

A2.....16.5 × 23.4 in (420 × 594 mm)

A3.....11.7 × 16.5 in (297 × 420 mm)

A4.....8.3 × 11.7 in (210 × 297 mm)

A5......5.8 × 8.3 in (148 × 210 mm)

A6......4.1 × 5.8 in (105 × 148 mm)

A7.........2.9 × 4.1 in (74 × 105 mm)

NON-OLYMPIC GAMES

Beetle herding • Bubble catching • Coin stacking
Competitive blinking • Competitive bumblebee throwing
Deep-sea eating • Endurance laughing • Stunt checkers
Heaviest-schoolbag carrying • Loudest-sneezing

———THE FIRST FIVE Gs OF ACCELERATION———

High acceleration and deceleration subject you to different experiences of gravity. The faster the rate of change in speed, the higher the g-force and the greater the effect on your body:

1-g   The effect of gravity on the surface of Earth—you feel this all the time.

2-g   The force you feel when you take off in an airplane. Your arms, legs, hands, and feet feel heavy.

3-g   The force you feel on a fast roller coaster. You are unable to lift your head to look around, and your heart has to work harder to pump blood around your body.

4-g   The force you feel in a relatively minor car crash. Your head feels four times heavier, and your neck muscles struggle to cope. Your vision narrows to a small tunnel. Colors fade to white, then to black.

5-g   The force felt by fighter pilots when they come out of an extremely fast turn. You may experience gravity-induced loss of consciousness, or g-loc.

———————WHICH IS A PERFECT CIRCLE?———————

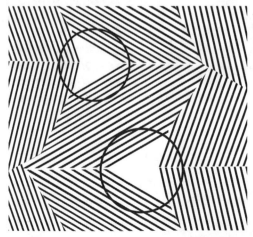

ANSWER: They both are.

DO YOU SEE IN 3-D?

Hold a finger upright in front of your face, then open and close one eye at a time. Your finger appears to jump to the side. That's because each eye views from a slightly different angle. Your brain blends the images together, and there you have it: a 3-D picture.

To test your 3-D vision, hold two pencils horizontally in front of you, level with your eyes. Slowly bring the tips of the two pencils together.

Easy? Now try repeating the exercise with one eye closed.

Closing one eye changes your vision to 2-D, so you can't tell which pencil is in the foreground and which is in the background.

HOW 3-D GLASSES WORK

One photograph is taken, and then the camera is moved slightly and another photograph is taken from a different angle.

Both photographs are printed on the same piece of paper, one image colored red and the other colored blue.

3-D glasses have one red and one blue lens. Looking through the red lens, the red picture seems to disappear so only the blue one can be seen, and vice versa. With each eye seeing a slightly different picture, the effect is 3-D.

YOGA POSES

Cow face • Bow • Bridge • Camel • Cat • Warrior
Downward-facing dog • One-legged king pigeon
Mountain • Half lord of the fishes • Corpse

——EXTROVERT—— OR ——INTROVERT?——

EXTROVERT	INTROVERT?
Outgoing	Reserved
Easygoing	Complicated
Thinks later	Thinks first
Emotional	Aloof
Changes the world	Understands the world
Breadth	Depth
Action	Ideas
Noise and variety	Quiet and concentration
Lots of people	One-on-one

——————ORIENTEERING MAP SYMBOLS——————

Orienteering maps are made for people who want to navigate an area on foot. Features of the landscape are shown in different colors:

Black..Rocks and man-made features

Brown..Landforms

Blue...Water features

Yellow..Easy-to-pass vegetation

Green..Difficult-to-pass vegetation

White....................................Forest with little or no undergrowth

Purple (or red)..The orienteering course

——————————MASS EXTINCTION——————————

Around 249 million years ago, 90 percent of all marine life and 70 percent of all land animals were wiped out, including dinosaurs. This mass extinction is thought to have been the result of either an asteroid impact or a massive environmental change.

—————————AN EASY METHOD—————————

You can use the following method (called a mnemonic) to remember the order of planets in our solar system: "My Vicious Earthworm Might Just Swallow Us Now." The first letter of each of the words corresponds to the first letter of one of the planets. Mercury is the planet closest to the Sun, and Neptune is the planet farthest away from the Sun.

My..Mercury

Vicious..Venus

Earthworm..Earth

Might...Mars

Just...Jupiter

Swallow..Saturn

Us...Uranus

Now..Neptune

—————————TEACHER, TEACHER—————————

Willy: "Teacher, teacher, do you think it's right to punish people for things they haven't done?"

Teacher: "Of course not."

Willy: "Good. I haven't done my homework."

Teacher: "You missed school yesterday, didn't you?"

Willy: "Not very much, no."

Teacher: "Why did you eat your homework, Willy?"

Willy: "You told me it was a piece of cake."

Teacher: "I wish you would pay a little attention."

Willy: "I can't pay anything. I didn't get my allowance this week."

SAILING TERMS

BROACHING
The boat suddenly tips in the water.

DEATH ROLL
The boat rolls from side to side until it either capsizes or the captain takes action.

HEELING
The strength of the wind makes the boat lean over.

HIKING
The crew leans over the edge of the boat as it heels, to stop it tipping over.

IN IRONS
The wind blows head-on and can push the boat backward.

JIBING
The boat's stern (rear) is turned through the wind so that the wind blows from the other side.

TACKING
The boat's bow (front) is turned through the wind so that the wind blows from the other side.

DON'T-GO ZONE
The wind blows from directly astern of (behind) the boat, making it really difficult to sail.

CAPSIZING
The boat overturns, so that the underside is on top.

---CONVERT IT---

inches (in)	$\xrightarrow{\times 2.54}$ $\xleftarrow{\times 0.3937}$	centimeters (cm)
feet (ft)	$\xrightarrow{\times 0.3048}$ $\xleftarrow{\times 3.2808}$	meters (m)
miles (mi)	$\xrightarrow{\times 1.6093}$ $\xleftarrow{\times 0.6214}$	kilometers (km)
square inches (sq in)	$\xrightarrow{\times 6.4516}$ $\xleftarrow{\times 0.155}$	square centimeters (cm^2)
square feet (sq ft)	$\xrightarrow{\times 0.0929}$ $\xleftarrow{\times 10.7639}$	square meters (m^2)
square miles (sq mi)	$\xrightarrow{\times 2.59}$ $\xleftarrow{\times 0.3861}$	square kilometers (km^2)
acres	$\xrightarrow{\times 0.4047}$ $\xleftarrow{\times 2.471}$	hectares
cubic inches (cu in)	$\xrightarrow{\times 16.3871}$ $\xleftarrow{\times 0.0613}$	cubic centimeters (cm^3)
pints	$\xrightarrow{\times 56.826}$ $\xleftarrow{\times 0.0176}$	centiliters (cl)
gallons (gal)	$\xrightarrow{\times 4.5460}$ $\xleftarrow{\times 0.22}$	liters (l)
ounces (oz)	$\xrightarrow{\times 28.3495}$ $\xleftarrow{\times 0.0353}$	grams (g)
pounds (lb)	$\xrightarrow{\times 0.454}$ $\xleftarrow{\times 2.2046}$	kilograms (kg)
tons (ton)	$\xrightarrow{\times 1016}$ $\xleftarrow{\times 0.001}$	kilograms (kg)

16 ounces = 1 pound
12 inches = 1 foot
2,240 pounds = 1 ton
8 pints = 1 gallon

100 centimeters = 1 meter
1,000 meters = 1 kilometer
1,000 grams = 1 kilogram
100 centiliters = 1 liter

────SEVEN PLAYGROUND HANDBALL TERMS────

1. *Baby*: Hitting the ball very softly so that it barely bounces off the wall—your opponent has to rush forward to hit it before it bounces twice.

2. *Catchie*: Catching the ball and throwing it rather than hitting it.

3. *Hardie*: Hitting the ball so hard that it lands behind the line of the court.

4. *Interference*: When your opponent gets in your way so you can't hit the ball.

5. *Out-of-bounds*: A ball that lands outside the square or court.

6. *Do-over*: Replaying a game. This happens when players disagree on whether a ball was out or not.

7. *Watermelon*: A ball that lands right at the spot where the wall meets the ground; sometimes called a *waterfall*.

──────────FICTIONAL SCHOOLS──────────

Starfleet Academy..*Star Trek*

Springfield Elementary...*The Simpsons*

Bedrock High School...*The Flintstones*

Xavier's School for Gifted Youngsters.......................................*X-Men*

Sunnydale High School................................*Buffy the Vampire Slayer*

Unseen University.....................................The Discworld novels

Midtown High School......................Spider-Man's school in the Bronx

Imperial Academy..*Star Wars*

Pokémon Battle Judge Training Institute................................*Pokémon*

Hogwarts School of Witchcraft and Wizardry................The Harry Potter novels

―――――――――SILLY SUPERHEROES―――――――――

INEDIBLE MAN
Though he is only the size of a marshmallow and smells good, he tastes completely disgusting. As soon as you pop him into your mouth, the gag reflex sends him shooting across the room to fight another day.

PETER-PIPER-PICKED-A-PECK-OF-PICKLED-PEPPERS MAN
"Oh no, it's Peter-Piper-Pecked-a-Pick . . . it's Peker-Piker-Kicked . . . no, it's Peper-Piper-Peped . . . Grrrrrrrrr!" He is neither fast nor strong, but bad guys lose their demonic enthusiasm when they stumble on this superhero's awkward name.

SMILE MAN
Smile Man has a disarming smile. When Smile Man smiles, everybody smiles. Even bad-tempered villains can't stop grinning.

―――――――――CAN YOU BUILD IT?―――――――――

————HOW TO MAKE A BALLOON SWORD————

1. Blow up a long, thin balloon so that it is not quite full of air. You should be able to easily twist the balloon.

2. Tie a secure knot at the bottom.

3. To make the handle of the sword, twist the balloon about 4 in (10 cm) up from the bottom. Make sure you keep hold of it, so that it doesn't untwist.

4. To form the crosspiece of the sword, make another twist about 3 in (8 cm) up from the first one. Then make a third twist the same distance from the second one.

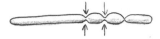

5. Twist the first and last twists together.

6. Twist this with the handle and let go. The first part of the crosspiece is now done and will stay in place.

7. Make two more twists, which are again 3 in (8 cm) apart, above the first part of the crosspiece.

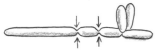

8. Twist the second twist around the first one to make the second part of the crosspiece.

9. Your sword is now complete!

MOON FACTS

The Moon is 2,160 miles (3,476 km) across.

The 238,855-mile (384,400-km) journey from Earth to the Moon takes a spaceship about two days. It would take an airplane about 26 days.

The Moon has no brightness of its own. It is lit up by the Sun.

There are dark spots on the Moon that early astronomers mistook for seas and lakes. In fact, they are dry surface features but have kept their watery names and are called things like "The Sea of Tranquility" and "The Lake of Sorrow."

SPOONERISMS

Spoonerisms are phrases where the first letters or sounds of words get mixed up through a slip of the tongue.

Pouring with rain..Roaring with pain

A pack of lies..A lack of pies

Take a shower..Shake a tower

Lighting a fire..Fighting a liar

Doing the chores..Chewing the doors

Funny bone..Bunny phone

HOOF HEARTED, ICE MELTED

Say this quickly:

One smart man, he felt smart. Two smart men, they felt smart. Three smart men, they all felt smart.

────── THE HISTORY OF SKATEBOARDING ──────

1950	Bored surfers invent a device called a "truck" that holds wheels to a board and allows a skater to steer the board by shifting his or her weight around.
1958	The first skateboards go on sale in a small surf shop in California.
1963	The first skate contest takes place at a school in Hermosa, California.
1965	Skateboarding booms, becomes mainstream, loses its cool, then dies out.
1970	The invention of "kick tail" boards and polyurethane wheels with bearings dramatically increases the maneuverability of skateboards, and the sport becomes popular again.
1978	Alan "Ollie" Gelfand performs the first "ollie," a skateboarding jump that almost all modern-day tricks are based on. Skaters can now jump over objects.
1981	The first edition of *Thrasher* magazine, a guide for underground skaters, is published.
1985	Vert-riding (skating on ramps and other vertical structures) and street-style skating become popular. Professional skaters start competing for big money.
1987	"New school" skating, with an emphasis on technical tricks, becomes popular.
1990s	A focus on street-style and new technology shapes skateboarding into the sport it is today.

────── WAYS TO BREAK A WEREWOLF CURSE ──────

Remove your animal-skin belt, in case it is enchanted.

Kneel in one spot for a hundred years.

Be saluted with the sign of the cross.

Be addressed three times by your baptismal name.

Be struck three times on the forehead with a knife, drawing
at least three drops of blood.

Get someone to throw an iron object at you.

──────HOW TO MAKE A BIRD FEEDER──────

You will need a large, open pinecone and ¼ cup each of crushed peanuts, sunflower seeds, oats, raisins, and mild grated cheese. You'll also need water and a length of string.

1. Mix the peanuts, sunflower seeds, oats, raisins, and cheese in a bowl.

2. Add a little water to your mixture to make it sticky.

3. Push the mixture into the gaps in the pinecone.

4. Tie a piece of string around the stuffed pinecone and hang it in your garden, ideally someplace where you can see it from a window.

5. It may take a while for the birds to pluck up the courage to visit your feeder, but be patient—they'll come around.

──────────DONKEY OR SEAL?──────────

──STRANGE THINGS SOLD ON THE INTERNET──

Secondhand false teeth • Half-eaten chocolate bar
A celebrity's chewed chewing gum • Toenail clippings
An empty cardboard box • A bottle of air
A potato-chip bag • A person's hand in marriage

GROSS FOOD RECORDS

LARGEST CUSTARD-PIE FIGHT
The world's largest custard-pie fight was fought in Bolton, England, on April 11, 2000. A total of 3,320 custard pies were thrown by two teams of ten people in three minutes.

FASTEST KETCHUP DRINKING
On September 23, 1999, Dustin Phillips of the United States drank 91 percent of a standard 13.9 oz (396 g) glass bottle of Heinz Tomato Ketchup through a drinking straw in 33 seconds.

MOST SAUSAGES SWALLOWED IN ONE MINUTE
On March 13, 2003, Cecil Walker of the United States swallowed eight whole sausages without chewing. Each sausage measured 16 inches (15 cm) in length and 0.87 inches (2.22 cm) in diameter.

MOST ICE CREAM EATEN IN 30 SECONDS
Diego Siu of the United States holds the record for eating the most ice cream in 30 seconds using a teaspoon. He consumed 9.3 oz (264 g) of vanilla ice cream in 30 seconds on March 2, 2003.

MOST BRUSSELS SPROUTS EATEN IN ONE MINUTE
Dave Mynard of the United Kingdom managed to eat 43 Brussels sprouts in one minute in London on December 10, 2003.

LONGEST PANCAKE MARATHON
On October 24, 1999, Mike Cuzzacrea flipped a pancake continually in a frying pan for just over three hours as he ran the 26.2-mile (40-km) New York Marathon.

─────ARE YOU A BORN CRIMINAL?─────

According to the theories of the 19th-century criminologist Cesare Lombroso (now debunked), there are 18 key physical indicators of the born criminal:

An unusually short or tall body
Long arms
Sloping shoulders, but large chest
Pointy or stubbed fingers or toes
Wrinkles on forehead and face
Beaked or flat nose
Large, protruding ears
Strong jawline
High cheekbones
Oversize incisors
Small or weak chin
Receding hairline
Small head, but large face
Small and sloping forehead
Fleshy lips or thin upper lip
Large eye sockets, but deep-set eyes
Bumps on back of head and around ear
Bushy eyebrows, tending to meet across nose

─────SMALL─────	─────LARGE─────
Petite • Mini	Massive • Big
Little • Teeny	Gargantuan • Giant
Tiny • Minuscule	Colossal • Huge
Diminutive • Wee	Enormous • Immense
Minute • Miniature	Gigantic • Monster
Microscopic • Baby	Vast • Whopping

─────HOW TO MAKE A GRASS WHISTLE─────

1. To find a suitable blade of grass, look for one that is long and at least a quarter of an inch wide.
2. Trap the blade of grass between the outer edges of your thumbs, pressed together, with the nails facing toward you.
3. You should be able to see the blade of grass in the gap just below the joints of your thumbs.
4. Press your lips to the gap and blow.
5. If you don't produce a whistle at first, keep adjusting the position of your lips and the grass until you get it right.

─────────SECRET SOCIETY OATH─────────

"I promise never to reveal the existence of the society to anyone else without first swearing them to the secret oath. I promise never to speak of the business of the society or to trade secrets with another society for personal gain. I promise never to reveal secret hiding places or code names. I swear this on all that is best kept secret."

─────CITIES WITH THE MOST UNDERGROUND───── RAILWAY LINES

New York...22
Paris, France..14
London, England...12
Madrid, Spain...12
Tokyo, Japan...12
Mexico City, Mexico..11
Moscow, Russia...11
Barcelona, Spain...9
Berlin, Germany...9
Seoul, South Korea..8

——REAL-LIFE—— DOUBLES

IMPERSONATOR
A person who mimics your voice and/or mannerisms.

POLITICAL DECOY
A person employed to impersonate a politician in order to draw attention away from them or to take risks on their behalf.

BODY DOUBLE
Someone who substitutes for an actor in dangerous scenes.

LOOK-ALIKE
A living person who closely resembles another person, often a celebrity, politician, or member of royalty.

——FOLKLORE—— DOUBLES

DOPPELGÄNGER
A spirit who looks exactly like you, but casts no shadow and has no reflection in a mirror or water.

SHADOWMAN
A black, humanlike silhouette that lacks a mouth or eyes. It appears on the edge of your field of vision and disintegrates when noticed.

EVIL TWIN
Exists in another dimension, but occasionally enters your world through a porthole. If you catch sight of it, you are in danger.

The eyes of a giant squid can be up to 15 inches (40 cm) wide.

─────────────── MADE INTO MUSICALS ───────────────

The sinking of the *Titanic*...*Titanic*

British prime minister Margaret Thatcher.....*Thatcher: The Musical*

TV show *Jerry Springer*............................*Jerry Springer: The Opera*

International cherry-pit-spit championship...............*Spittin' Distance*

The electric chair...*Fields of Ambrosia*

─────────────── SUN FACTS ───────────────

The Sun is the star at the center of our solar system.

It is a huge ball of hydrogen and helium gas.

Earth is 93 million miles (150 million km) from the Sun.

You could fit over a million Earths into the Sun.

All the planets of our solar system, including Earth,
orbit the Sun.

The Sun is approximately 400 times wider than Earth's Moon.
The reason they appear to be about the same size is that
the Sun is 400 times farther away from us.

The temperature at the Sun's core is about
28,100,000°F (16,600,000°C).

The Sun's heat and light support almost all life on Earth.

The Sun's lifetime is predicted to be around 10 billion years.
At the moment it is about 4.5 billion years old.

─────────────── UNCOMMON CITRUS FRUITS ───────────────

Ugli fruit • Buddha's hand • Dekopon
Rough lemon • Calamanci • Kumquat
Limequat • Pomelo • Ponkan • Limetta • Natsumikan

───────HOW TO WRITE A LIMERICK───────

A limerick is a poem with a very specific structure. Limericks traditionally start with "There once was a . . ." and are made up of five lines. The first, second, and fifth lines have eight syllables, and the last syllables of each one should rhyme. The third and fourth lines have five syllables and a different rhyme.

1. Think of a character you would like to write about and give it a name. Now write an eight-syllable sentence ending with that name. For example:
   There once was a lion called Len,

2. Think of as many words as you can that rhyme with the name you have chosen. Select one to go at the end of the second eight-syllable line, so that the story is continued. For example:
   Who lived in a quaint, cozy den.

3. Now write the next two lines. Remember that these are made up of five syllables and should have a different rhyme. For example:
   He liked to stay in,
   And open a tin.

4. Now finish off your limerick. The last line is another eight-syllable line. It should rhyme with the first two lines and finish off your story.
   And never went hunting again.

───────ANIMALS IN ORDER OF INTELLIGENCE───────

1. Human	8. Whale
2. Chimpanzee	9. Dolphin
3. Gorilla	10. Elephant
4. Orangutan	11. Pig
5. Baboon	12. Dog
6. Gibbon	13. Cat
7. Monkey	14. Octopus

THE DREADED KRAKEN

Sailors beware the fabled sea monster known as the Kraken. The monster's immense, rounded back resembles an island. Desperate for dry land, sea-weary sailors have been known to drop anchor and row out to it. Before settling down for a night's rest, the fires are lit—at which point the Kraken wakes up. The unfortunate sailors are drowned. Or worse.

APPLE-SEED FORTUNES

Cut an apple in half. The number of seeds you see will tell you your fortune.

One seed	Good luck
Two seeds	Marriage
Three seeds	Wealth
Four seeds	Travel
Five seeds	Health
Six seeds	Wisdom
Seven seeds	Fame

---TRACE THE SHAPES---

Shapes that can be traced in one continous line, without taking your pencil off the page and without tracing along any line twice:

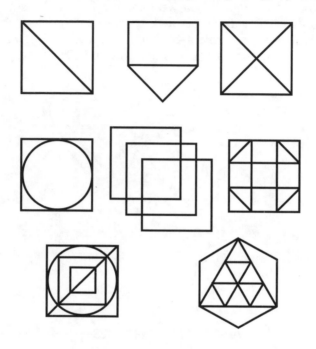

---A GRUESOME EXECUTION---

In 1757, the execution of Robert-François Damiens, who attempted to assassinate the French king Louis XV, began with torture using red-hot pincers. The hand with which he'd held a knife was then burned off using sulfur. Next, molten wax, lead, and boiling oil were poured into his wounds. Horses were then harnessed to his arms and legs and made to run in opposite directions, so that his limbs would rip off. But his joints wouldn't tear, so the executioner had to cut through them with a knife. Even after all this agonizing torture, Damiens was rumored not to have died, and his head and torso were later burned at the stake.

THE POLES

The North and South Poles are the points at which Earth's axis of rotation meets Earth's surface.

THE NORTH POLE

The exact North Pole, called the Geographic North Pole, is located in the Arctic Ocean. In whichever direction you travel from the Geographic North Pole, you are always heading south.

Magnetic North is the place to which all magnetic compasses point. It is not the same point as the Geographic North Pole.

The North Pole has 24 hours of daylight during the summer months and 24 hours of darkness during the winter months.

THE SOUTH POLE

The exact South Pole, called the Geographic South Pole, is located on the continent of Antarctica. In whichever direction you travel from the Geographic South Pole, you are always heading north.

The Ceremonial South Pole is an area set aside for photo opportunities a few hundred feet from the Geographic South Pole.

The ice cap at the South Pole is 9,840 ft (3,000 m) thick, but the ice is melting. Over 8,000 square miles (13,000 square km) of sea ice have been lost in Antarctica over the last 50 years. This is generally thought to be the consequence of global warming.

---SURF SPEAK---

Dawn patrol.................................Getting up early for a morning surf

Regular footer.............................Surfer who rides left-foot forward

Goofy footer..............................Surfer who rides right-foot forward

Kook...Hopeless surfer

Dude..Anyone and everyone

Beach breaks...Constant waves

Point breaks...Perfect waves

Gnarly.............................The sea when the waves are very choppy

Shredding..Surfing like a pro

Aerial........................Jumping your board into the air above a wave

Wicked drop-in................................Stealing another person's wave

Insane...Anything that's cool

Stoked..Really happy

Surfed out..In need of a rest

---TOO MUCH TV---

Goggle eyes • TV addict • Square eyes • Couch potato
Sofa sloth • Technicolor dreamer

————————————— CURSED ———————————————

THE CURSE OF THE PHARAOHS

There is a belief that any person who disturbs the tomb of an ancient Egyptian pharaoh will die shortly afterward. The curse struck the team who opened the tomb of Pharaoh Tutankhamen in 1922. Within 6 years of the tomb's discovery, 12 of the archaeologists were dead, including the expedition's patron, Lord Carnarvon, who died 47 days after entering the tomb.

THE HOPE DIAMOND

Part of the French crown jewels worn by Marie Antoinette at her execution, the diamond is thought to bring bad luck to whoever possesses it. Owners have met their deaths as a result of suicides, car crashes, and cliff falls.

ANCIENT ROMAN CURSES

The ancient Romans had a formula for making an enemy suffer an injury. They wrote curses on lead tablets, known as *tabulae defixiones*, and put them in a tomb or a sacred spring.

TECUMSEH'S CURSE

Between 1840 and 1960, all the U.S. presidents elected in the years divisible by 20 died in office. This is said to stem from a curse issued by the Indian chief Tecumseh in 1811, when General William Henry Harrison defeated Tecumseh in battle and won the presidency. Harrison caught a cold and died having spent just one month in office. The curse was broken by Ronald Reagan, elected in 1980, who survived an assassin's bullet by less than an inch.

————————— SCAMMER'S LANGUAGE —————————

Con or scam...........An attempt to trick someone out of something

Grifter..The con artist

Mark or pigeon..The victim

Shill................................A grifter's accomplice who pretends to be just a member of the public

──────── HOW TO MAKE A WATER CLOCK ────────

Here is a simple method for making a time-keeping device.

1. Cut the top off a plastic 2-liter bottle, about 3 inches (8 cm) from the top.

2. Stick a strip of masking tape on the outside of the bottle, so that it runs in a straight line from the top to the bottom.

3. Make a small hole in the bottom of a paper cup and fit the cup snugly into the opening you cut at the top of the bottle.

4. Have a stopwatch ready in front of you. Fill the cup with water. The moment you start pouring, start the stopwatch.

5. Every minute, mark the water level on the masking tape. Always make sure the paper cup is at least half full with water, so that it runs into the bottle in a steady stream.

6. Once the bottle is filled with water and you've made all the markings, you can use the "clock" to keep track of the time.

──REAL PARTS── OF A SWISS ARMY KNIFE	──PARTS OF A── SWISS ARMY KNIFE NOT YET INVENTED
Large blade	Skeleton key
Small blade	Grappling hook
Corkscrew	Pea-shooter
Can opener	Industrial laser
Small screwdriver	Bugging device
Bottle opener	Miniature fishing reel
Pliers	Universal remote control
Tweezers	Digital voice recorder
Flashlight	Invisible-ink pen
Scissors	Telescope

SYMMETRICAL WORDS

If you were to draw a horizontal line through the middle of the following words, the tops of the words would be mirror images of the bottoms:

COOKBOOK	BIKED
EXCEEDED	DICED
HOODED	CHOKE
DEED	CHOICE
BEDECKED	HIKED
CHEEK	BOBBED

THE OLDEST EVER

Marine clam	200 years old
Human	122 years old
Elephant	78 years old
Giant tortoise	75 years old
Horse	62 years old
Dog	29 years old
Mouse	4 years old

It takes just ¹/₅₀ of a second for the guillotine blade to sever the head from the neck, though it has been suggested that it may take up to 7 seconds for the brain to lose consciousness after the head is severed.

---IS THIS ART?---

Some important modern pieces of art have included:

A urinal
A pile of bricks
An unmade bed
A garbage can
A black canvas
A sheep cut in half
A wrapped-up dog kennel
An empty room with a
lightbulb that repeatedly
goes on and off

---HOW TO MAKE A COMPASS---

You will need a clear glass bowl filled with water, a 0.2-in (0.5-cm) slice from the end of a cork, a magnet, and a needle.

1. Float the cork in the bowl of water.

2. Magnetize the needle by rubbing it over the magnet in the same direction about 50 times.

3. Lay the needle on the cork.

The needle will slowly turn to line up with Earth's North and South Magnetic Poles.

---LOUDEST-EVER HUMAN NOISES---

Knuckle crack...........108 decibels, Bob Hatch, USA, May 17, 2000

Burp................................118.1 decibels, Paul Hunn, UK, April 5, 2000

Scream.....................129 decibels, Jill Drake, UK, October 22, 2000

———— HOW TO CHART YOUR FAMILY TREE ————

1. Write your name at the bottom of a large piece of paper.

2. If you have any brothers or sisters, write their names alongside yours, oldest on the left, youngest on the right.

3. Draw a vertical line out of the top of each of the names. Finish each line at the same point, then join the top of the lines together with a horizontal line.

4. Draw a vertical line upward from the center of the horizontal line.

5. Starting at the top of the vertical line, draw a short horizontal line to either side.

6. Write your father's name on the left of the line and your mother's name on the right. Your family tree should now look something like this:

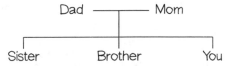

7. Write the names of your father's brothers and sisters to the left of his name, and your mother's brothers and sisters to the right of her name, in age order from left to right.

8. Connect the names of the brothers and sisters in your father's family, and draw a vertical line to the names of their parents (your grandparents) in the same way you connected the names of the children in your family to your parents. Now do the same for your mother's side of the family.

9. Write the names of your grandparents' brothers and sisters next to your grandparents' names, and connect them to the names of their parents (your great-grandparents).

10. Continue this pattern to trace your family tree as far back as you can—ask your relatives to help you find out all the names. You may also wish to add everyone's dates of birth.

HOMEMADE INSTRUMENTS

DRUMS
Stretch different materials (such as plastic bags or balloons)
tightly over pots of different sizes, using rubber bands, and
strike with a soup spoon.

MARACAS
Fill a plastic water bottle or film canister with
rice, pebbles, coffee beans, or sand. Vitamin containers
are ready-made maracas.

CYMBALS
Bang two saucepan lids together.

XYLOPHONES
Fill drinking glasses or glass bottles with varying amounts
of water and line them up from most to least full. Tap
each glass with a pencil to produce different notes.

The ancient Greek mathematician Hero invented
the vending machine in Alexandria. The coin
dropped onto a lever, which opened a valve, and
out flowed a small amount of holy water.

─────── TIPS FOR AVOIDING BEE STINGS ───────

1. Never try to swat a honeybee. Bees are generally passive unless annoyed or threatened and usually sting only in self-defense.

2. Smell horrible. Bees like flowers that smell nice. You stink, they fly away.

3. Wear camouflage. Bees have poor eyesight and won't be able to spot you if you are wearing light colors in the day or dark colors at night.

4. Never mow the lawn. The low buzzing of motorized garden tools can agitate swarms, hives, or colonies.

5. Keep your shoes on. Particularly avoid walking barefoot over lawns that contain blooming clover, which bees love.

6. If a bee head-butts you, move quickly in the opposite direction. Sentry bees patrolling the edges of the hive's territory do this to warn off invaders.

7. Stay indoors until sunset. Bees generally sleep after dark.

─────── THE SPEED YOU MAKE THE AIR MOVE ───────

Inhaling...4 mph (6 kph)

Sniffing...20 mph (30 kph)

Coughing...60 mph (100 kph)

Sneezing..100 mph (160 kph)

─────── RETIRED HURRICANE NAMES ───────

All hurricanes are given a name from a long list. If an unusually destructive hurricane hits, its name is retired and never used again. Among those retired are:

Allison • Andrew • Floyd • Georges • Katrina
Keith • Iris • Lenny • Michelle

THINGS THAT PROBABLY AREN'T GOING TO HAPPEN TO YOU

Dying in a fireworks accident.............................odds are 1,000,000 to 1

Being killed by lightning..odds are 2,300,000 to 1

Dying from food poisoning...................................odds are 3,000,000 to 1

Seeing a UFO...odds are 3,000,000 to 1

Getting hit by parts falling off an airplane....odds are 10,000,000 to 1

Becoming president...odds are 10,000,000 to 1

Becoming a saint..odds are 20,000,000 to 1

Getting mad cow disease....................................odds are 40,000,000 to 1

Being killed by a shark......................................odds are 300,000,000 to 1

A meteor landing on your house....odds are 182,138,880,000,000 to 1

THE LONGEST-EVER HAIRS

Longest eyebrow............................3.07 in (7.81 cm), Franklin Ames, USA

Longest leg hair..............................4.8 in (12.4 cm), Tim Stinton, Australia

Longest ear hair........................5.2 in (13.2 cm), Radhakant Bajpai, India

Longest female beard..................11 in (27.9 cm), Vivian Wheeler, USA

---STICK PUZZLE---

Take away nine sticks to form only four squares.
All squares (large and small) are counted, and each
stick must be part of a square.

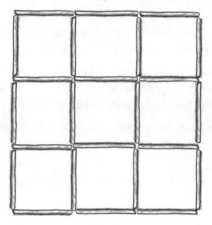

Answer on page 120.

---HOW TO PLAY CUPS---

1. This is a game to be played in a swimming pool, lake, or the ocean. Two players stand back-to-back in waist-deep water.

2. Choose one player to be the cupper and one player to be the guesser.

3. At the count of three, both players must duck under water. The cupper then swims one stroke either to the left or to the right. At the same time, the guesser swims one stroke in the direction that he or she thinks the cupper has swum.

4. If, when both players resurface, they are in the same place, the guesser has guessed correctly and takes the point. If they are two strokes apart, the cupper has outsmarted the guesser and the cupper takes the point.

5. After three games, the player with the most wins takes the role of the cupper.

─────────THE OFFSIDE RULE IN SOCCER─────────

The offside rule is said to be soccer's most complicated rule. Understanding the rule traditionally distinguishes real soccer fans from everyone else.

An attacking player is in an offside position if he or she is nearer his or her opponents' goal line than both the ball and the last defender (not including the goalie).

However, the player is penalized for being in an offside position only if his or her team gains an advantage from it at the moment the ball is played by one of his or her teammates.

When defenders deliberately move forward to try to put an attacker offside, it is known as the "offside trap."

There is no offense if the offside player receives the ball directly from a goal kick, throw-in, or corner kick.

If you get stuck in the middle of your spaceship in zero gravity and are unable to reach the floor, ceiling, or walls, do not despair. Instead, take off a shoe and throw it across the cabin. You and your shoe will act as a pair of equal and opposite forces, propelling you backward. The harder you throw your shoe, the faster you will be pushed away from it.

─────────EMBARRASSED AT SCHOOL─────────

Your mom kisses you good-bye at the school entrance.

Your sister follows you, calling you by your family nickname.

You get chosen last when picking teams for P.E.

Your parents make friends with the parents of the school geek, and they arrange for you all to go on vacation together.

There's a stink in the bathroom. Everyone's talking about it, and you're responsible.

-------FAMOUS LAST WORDS-------

THE SCIENTIST
The 19th-century British surgeon Joseph Henry Green checked his own pulse, announced "Stopped," and then died.

THE POET
The German poet Heinrich Heine never got to give his last message to the world, his final words being "Write . . . write . . . pencil . . . paper."

THE PLAYWRIGHT
The Norwegian dramatist Henrik Ibsen heard his nurse tell a visitor that he was feeling better. "On the contrary," Ibsen said, and died.

THE ACTOR
Hollywood swashbuckler Douglas Fairbanks declared "I've never felt better" and promptly died.

THE PHILOSOPHER
The German political philosopher Karl Marx was asked by his maid if he had any last words. He replied, "Go on, get out! Last words are for fools who haven't said enough!"

THE WIT
The last words of Oscar Wilde are believed to be: "Either this wallpaper goes, or I do."

You can't stop yourself from vomiting by keeping your mouth shut. The vomit will just come out of your nose instead.

—HOW NOT TO GET EATEN BY A POLAR BEAR—

1. Bears hate noise. So if you see one nearby, shout and
   scream out as loud as you can to keep it at bay.

2. If a polar bear approaches you, always act in a non-
   threatening manner. Lower your eyes to the ground, avoiding
   eye-contact, and back slowly away.

3. If the bear continues to approach, stand your ground, hold
   your arms over your head (or better still your coat) to make
   yourself look bigger, and make more noise.

——FAKE HARRY POTTER BOOKS IN CHINA——

Harry Potter and the Porcelain Doll
Harry Potter and the Leopard-Walk-Up-to-Dragon
Harry Potter and the Golden Turtle
Harry Potter and the Crystal Vase

—RIDDLE—

What do astronauts drink?

Gravi-tea

——— CLOTHING SIZES AROUND THE WORLD ———

WOMEN'S CLOTHES

American	8	10	12	14	16	18
British	10	12	14	16	18	20
Continental	38	40	42	44	46	48

MEN'S CLOTHES

American	36	38	40	42	44	46
British	36	38	40	42	44	46
Continental	46	48	50	52	54	56

CHILDREN'S CLOTHES

American	4	6	8	10	12	14
British						
Height (in)	36	38	40	42	44	46
Age	4–5	6–8	9–10	11	12	13
Continental						
Height (cm)	125	135	150	155	160	165
Age	7	9	12	13	14	15

> Army ants of South America don't have nests. They live on the move, foraging as they go. Anything in their path, including animals, is likely to be eaten alive.

——— A LIGHTBULB PROBLEM ———

You are in a room with three light switches labeled 1, 2, 3. One of the light switches controls a bulb you can't see that is in the next room. All three switches are off and the lightbulb is off. You can flick any of the switches as many times as you want, for as long as you want. You can then go into the next room once to check the bulb. How will you find out which switch is connected to the bulb?

Answer: Turn switch 1 on for 10 minutes, then turn it off. Turn switch 2 on, then immediately go to check the bulb. If it is off and hot, it is switch 1. If it is on, it is switch 2. If it is off and cold, it is switch 3.

——CHRISTMAS DINNERS AROUND THE WORLD——

Turkey...Salted dry cod with boiled potatoes

Transylvania...Stuffed cabbage

Russia...Meat dumplings

Sweden............Baked ham, pickled herring, lutfish and rice pudding

Poland...............................Beetroot soup, prune dumplings, carp

Britain...Roasted goose

Germany...Carp or goose

USA...Roasted turkey

——————————ONE YEAR IN SPACE——————————

A year is the amount of time it takes
a planet to go around the Sun.

PLANET	DISTANCE FROM SUN (million miles)	LENGTH OF YEAR (in Earth days)
Mercury	36	88
Venus	67	225
Earth	93	365
Mars	142	687
Jupiter	484	4,333
Saturn	887	10,750
Uranus	1,784	30,707
Neptune	2,796	60,202

> The one-syllable word *are* can be
> changed into a three-syllable word by
> adding the single letter *a* to the end of it.

REALLY LONG WALKS

THE MEDIEVAL PILGRIMAGE
Medieval pilgrims walked 1,000 miles (1,600 km) from France to reach the holy shrine in Santiago de Compostela, Spain.

THE APPALACHIAN TRAIL
This 2,167-mile (3,487-km) trail through the Appalachian Mountains of United States is the longest hiking trail in the world.

THE SILK ROAD
In 100 B.C., Chinese silk merchants traveled 3,700 miles (6,000 km) along the Silk Road from China to Imperial Rome.

THE GREAT WALL OF CHINA
Also known as "the longest graveyard on Earth," this ancient fortification stretches 1,500 miles (2,400 km) through scorching deserts, mountains, and dangerous forests.

HOW WATERY?

A tomato	95 percent
A potato	80 percent
A human	75 percent
A loaf of bread	35 percent

————THE FORMING OF THE CONTINENTS————

By looking at the structure of Earth, it is possible to form theories about how the continents we have today came into being.

YEARS AGO	CONTINENTS
3 billion	There was one continent called Ur
	which split into
2.5 billion	Ur and Arctica
	which split into
2 billion	Ur, Arctica, Baltica, and Atlantica
	then Arctica and Baltica joined to form Nena, so the continents were
1.5 billion	Nena, Ur, and Atlantica
	then Nena, Ur, and Atlantica joined to form
1 billion	Rodinia
	which split into
700 million	Nena, Atlantica, and Ur
	which joined again to form
300 million	Pangaea
	which eventually split into
200 million	Africa, Antarctica, Australia, Europe, Asia, and North and South America

————GREETINGS IN DIFFERENT COUNTRIES————

Japan..............Bow from the waist, palms on thighs, heels together

France...A kiss on both cheeks

New Zealand Maori...A touching of noses

Britain...A handshake

India...With palms pressed together as though praying, a bend or nod

MAJOR RISKS OF SPACE TRAVEL

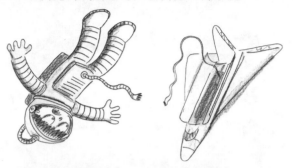

Becoming separated from the ship during a space-walk
Blacking out during takeoff
Crash-landing on an airless planet
Being hit by a meteor
Being exposed to radiation
Burning up on reentering the Earth's atmosphere

EINSTEIN'S PUZZLE

Three dragons, Dudley, Delilah, and Dave, live in three separate holes, numbered 1, 2, 3 from left to right. They each have a favorite rock band (The Scaly Singers, The Winged Wonders, and The Fire Breathers) and a favorite ice cream flavor (vanilla, strawberry, and chocolate). Based on the following information, which dragon loves chocolate ice cream and which dragon listens to The Scaly Singers?

Dudley loves vanilla ice cream.

Delilah's favorite rock band is The Fire Breathers.

The dragon that lives in the left hole is a fan of
The Winged Wonders.

Dudley and Delilah have one hole separating them.

The Scaly Singers fan does not live on the left of
the strawberry ice-cream lover.

ANSWER: Delilah loves chocolate ice cream. Dave listens to The Scaly Singers.

SHADOW PUPPETS

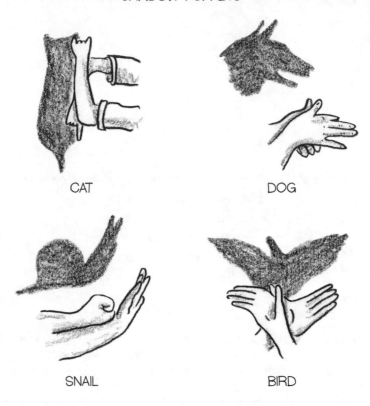

CAT

DOG

SNAIL

BIRD

GALILEO'S SHIP

You are in a cabin below the deck of a ship. You have with you two goldfish in a bowl, a ball, and a stick of incense. When the boat is at anchor, the goldfish swim with equal effort in all directions, the ball falls straight down from your hand to the floor, and the incense smoke drifts directly upward into the air. When the boat is moving in a straight line and at an even pace, will these effects change?

ANSWER: No. Everything contained in the ship, including the air, is moving at the same rate.

---HIGH-DIVING---

BACKWARD
The diver takes off with his or her back to the water.

PIKE
The body is folded in half, bent at the waist but not at the knees.

LAYOUT
The body is completely straight.

TUCK
The body is curled into a ball, with the knees brought up to the chin and the heels tucked against the backs of the legs.

WATER ENTRANCE
The diver must be straight, powerful, and make a minimal splash.

The world's highest-ever dive, a double-back somersault from 177 feet (54 m), was performed by the Swiss diver Oliver Favre in Villers-le-Lac, France, in 1987.

In 1998, the Swiss diver Frederic Weill performed a dive from a helicopter into Lake Verbano in Italy. The 86-foot (26-m) dive included an arm-stand takeoff and double somersault pike.

The highest-ever shallow dive was performed by Danny Higginbottom from Louisiana, on September 8, 2004. He dived from a height of 29 feet, 4 inches (8.95 m) into 1 foot (30 cm) of water.

> Camels' humps do not contain water, as is commonly believed, but instead store fatty tissue that can be converted to water. The fat supply is enough for them to survive without a drink for about two weeks, and without food for up to a month.

EGYPTIAN HIEROGLYPHS

Ancient Egyptians wrote using hieroglyphics—a script made up of pictures. There are few clues as to how Egyptians pronounced their words, but here are some hieroglyphs that roughly translate to the letters of our alphabet (there is no equivalent for *c* or *x*).

a	b	d	e
as in *ant*	as in *bat*	as in *dad*	as in *eat*

f	g	h	i	j
as in *fog*	as in *got*	as in *hat*	as in *pin*	as in *jump*

k	l	m	n	o
as in *kite*	as in *lot*	as in *mum*	as in *not*	as in *who*

p	q	r	s	t
as in *pin*	as in *quit*	as in *run*	as in *sit*	as in *top*

u	v	w	y	z
as in *glue*	as in *van*	as in *wig*	as in *baby*	as in *zoo*

WHAT KIND OF -PHILE ARE YOU?

-phile is the opposite of *-phobe*
and means "loving."

Turophile...Cheese

Hippophile...Horses

Ophiophile...Snakes

Nyctophile..Darkness

Hoplophile...Weaponry

Xylophile..Wood

Logophile..Words

Technophile...Technology

Claustrophile...Enclosed spaces

Thalassophile...Seas

Francophile..France

Bibliophile..Books

TYPES OF FIREWORKS

Bottle rockets • Roman candles • Cones • Skyrockets
Pinwheels • Helicopters • Flares • Fountains • Cakes • Mines
Parachutes • Snappers • Voodoo balls • Flying satellites

WHAT'S THE DIFFERENCE?

INDIAN AND AFRICAN ELEPHANTS
The African elephant is larger than the Indian elephant and has larger ears. The African elephant has two lips on its trunk, while the Indian elephant has only one.

STALAGMITES AND STALACTITES
These icicle-shaped pillars form over thousands of years where water drips through the roof of a limestone cave, leaving mineral deposits behind. Stalagmites grow up from the ground, while stalactites grow down from the roof of the cave.

INTERNET AND THE WORLD WIDE WEB
The Internet is a massive network in which any computer can communicate with any other computer as long as they are both connected to the Internet. The World Wide Web is just one way of accessing information on the Internet. It uses a computer-programming language called HTTP. This is just one of the many languages used over the Internet.

COCA-COLA AND PEPSI-COLA
Coca-Cola was invented in 1886, followed by Pepsi in 1898. It is assumed that Coca-Cola was named after the coca leaves and kola nuts used to make it. Pepsi was named after the beneficial effects it was believed to have on a kind of bellyache called dyspepsia.

MONOPOLY RECORDS

Longest anti-gravitational game (played on the ceiling)....36 hours

Longest game played in a bath.....................................99 hours

Longest game played in an elevator............................16 days

Longest game played under water................................45 days

Longest game ever played...70 days

A KNOT TRICK

This is a handy trick to have up your sleeve if you want to win a bet. Tell your friends to try and tie a knot in a piece of string without letting go of the ends. They won't be able to do it. Follow this guide to show them how it's done.

With a piece of string on a table in front of you, cross your arms, as shown. One hand should be on top of the opposite arm and the other hand tucked under the opposite armpit.

Holding this position, lean forward and pick up one end and then the other, so you have an end of the string in each hand.

Now simply uncross your arms.

You'll be left with a neat knot in the center of the string.

Ostriches can run at 45 mph (72 kph) for nearly 20 minutes at a time.

——HOW TO EAT IN A FANCY RESTAURANT——

Sit up straight and keep your elbows off the table at all times. Be polite to the waitstaff. It simply isn't cool to boss people around. Always wait until everyone has been served before you start eating. Before drinking some water, make sure you have swallowed all the food in your mouth, then wipe your mouth with your napkin and take a sip. When you have finished your meal, place your napkin on the table, but do not fold it.

Now what not to do... Don't chew gum during the meal or burp at the table. Never pick up your soup bowl and drink from it. Never lick your knife. And never spit out any food you don't like, however horrible it is.

——————THE LARGEST COUNTRIES——————

Russia............................6,592,735 square miles (17,075,200 square km)

Canada............................3,851,788 square miles (9,976,140 square km)

China............................3,705,386 square miles (9,596,960 square km)

USA............................3,618,764 square miles (9,372,610 square km)

Brazil............................3,286,470 square miles (8,511,965 square km)

Australia............................2,967,893 square miles (7,686,850 square km)

---WORLD STANDARDS---

METER

A meter was originally a French standard of measurement. It was said to be one ten-millionth of the distance from the North Pole to the equator, when measured on a straight line running along the surface of Earth through Paris. Today, a meter is the distance traveled by light in a vacuum during 1/299,792,458 of a second.

FATHOM

Sailors used to measure the depth of water using a long, weighted rope called a sounding line. A fathom was the length of rope that a man could hold between his extended arms as he hauled it out of the sea. One fathom is 6 feet (1.8 m) long. In old English, the word *fathom* means "outstretched arm."

MILE

Roman soldiers kept track of the distances they marched by counting their paces. One pace was a double step. One mile was a thousand paces—in Latin, *mille passas*.

What is a robot's favorite part of the school day?

Assembly

---LIZARD NAMES---

Alectrosaurus..Unrelated lizard

Deinodon...Terrible tooth

Gasosaurus...Gas lizard

Nanosaurus...Dwarf lizard

Quaesitosaurus...Uncommon lizard

Saichania..Beautiful one

Ultrasaurus..Ultra-giant lizard

Xenotarsosaurus...Strange-ankle lizard

HOW TO MAKE A
BAKING SODA AND VINEGAR ROCKET

1. Get a plastic bottle.

2. Put about one inch of vinegar into the bottle.

3. Put a tablespoon of baking soda in a plastic bag.

4. Seal the bag and put it into the bottle.

5. Shake the bottle for 5 to 10 seconds.

6. Throw it down onto the pavement and well away from yourself.

A camel-hair brush is made of squirrel fur.

TEXTOGRAMS

Textograms are different words formed from the same number sequence on a telephone keypad. They are often mixed up when texting.

269...boy, box, cow
4663................................home, good, gone, hood, hoof
328..fat, eat
7664..snog, song
2253................................bake, cake, bald, calf
5693..love, loud

--------RIVERS, FROM SOURCE TO SEA--------

THE NILE
Source: Lake Victoria, east-
central Africa
Sea: Mediterranean Sea
Journey: 4,160 miles (6,695 km)

THE MISSISSIPPI
Source: Lake Itasca,
Minnesota
Sea: Gulf of Mexico
Journey: 2,302 miles (3,705 km)

THE GANGES
Source: Himalayan Mountains
Sea: Indian Ocean
Journey: 1,560 miles (2,510 km)

THE THAMES
Source: Cotswolds, England
Sea: North Sea
Journey: 210 miles (340 km)

THE AMAZON
Source: Andes Mountains,
Peru
Sea: Atlantic Ocean
Journey: 3,899 miles (6,275 km)

THE YANGTZE
Source: Kunlun Mountains,
western China
Sea: Pacific Ocean
Journey: 3,915 miles (6,300 km)

THE RHINE
Source: Swiss Alps
Sea: North Sea
Journey: 820 miles (1,320 km)

THE DANUBE
Source: Black Forest, Germany
Sea: Black Sea
Journey: 1,771 miles (2,850 km)

--------WHICH MIDDLE CIRCLE IS BIGGEST?--------

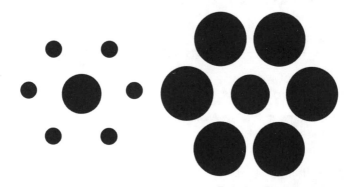

ANSWER: They are both the same size.

FUN RACES

INDIVIDUAL EVENTS

EGG-AND-SPOON RACE: The competitor must complete the race without dropping a hard-boiled egg balanced on a spoon.

PANCAKE RACE: At certain points in the race, the competitor must successfully flip a pancake in the frying pan he or she is running with.

SACK RACE: The competitor places both legs inside a sack and hops or shuffles to the finishing line.

PARTNER EVENTS

THREE-LEGGED RACE: The competitors tie their inside legs together and run in tandem.

PIGGYBACK RACE: The lighter competitor climbs on the heavier or stronger competitor's back and is carried to the finish line.

WHEELBARROW RACE: One competitor runs on his or her hands while the other follows behind holding his or her teammate's legs in the air.

LIFE ON MARS

The surface of Mars is thought to be mainly composed of a black volcanic rock called basalt, which is also found on Earth.

In December 1984, a Martian meteorite was found in Antarctica. It is thought to have contained fossils of microscopic bacteria that lived on Mars millions of years ago.

In 2004, the orbiting probe *Mars Express* found methane in the Martian atmosphere. On Earth, methane is emitted by primitive life forms.

TV FIRSTS

1926 Scottish engineer John Logie Baird gives the first public demonstration of a working television set in London.

1951 The world's first color TV show is broadcast in the United States. It is a musical variety show.

1955 The first wireless remote control is launched. It is called the Zenith Flash-matic.

1964 The plasma display monitor is invented.

1967 The first video game for a television set is launched. It is called *Chase*.

1969 A camera in the lunar module provides live television coverage as Neil Armstrong becomes the first man to walk on the Moon. Approximately 600 million people tune in.

1975 Sony launches the Betamax home-recording system. The system allows consumers to record and play back television shows.

1975 The band Queen produces the first successful pop video to the song "Bohemian Rhapsody."

1976 The Japanese company JVC launches the VHS home-recording system to rival Sony's Betamax.

1996 The first DVD players and discs are sold in Japan.

SPY CODE

Ears Only.........................Documents too secret to commit to writing

Eyes Only...............Documents that may be read but not discussed

Wet Job...An operation in which blood is shed

Dead Drop........................Secret location where messages are left

Black Operations..........Secret operations that no one owns up to

Mole...An agent sent to gather intelligence by working or living among the enemy

———WHO IS THE PATRON SAINT OF WHAT?———

Maria Goretti	Girls
John Bosco	Boys
Roch	Dogs
Francis of Assisi	Animals
Gabriel of Our Lady of Sorrows	Students
Amand	Scouts
Joseph of Cupertino	Astronauts
Fiacre	Taxi drivers
Isidore of Seville	Computer programmers
Clare of Assisi	Television
Barbara	Fireworks
Francis de Sales	Teachers

———THE PERPETUALLY ASCENDING STAIRCASE———

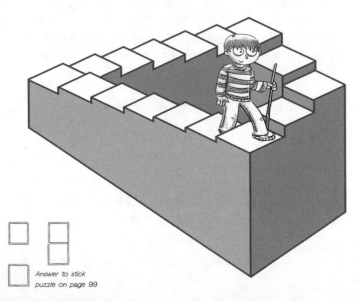

Answer to stick
puzzle on page 99

─────────ARE YOU TELEPATHIC?─────────

1. Get a friend to sit in front of you with a pack of playing cards.

2. Ask him or her to pick one card at random, without letting you see it. Then tell him or her to concentrate really hard on that card.

3. Close your eyes and empty your mind, allowing your brain to "receive" your friend's telepathic message.

4. Shout out the number and suit of the first card that comes to mind and see if you are correct.

In May 2005, a U.S. hot-dog company made a 75-foot (22.9-m) long hot dog, some 120 times longer than your average sausage.

─────────MEDIEVAL WEAPONS─────────

Knight's sword..............................Single-handed, cross-shaped sword

Claymore.........................Large, two-handed sword used in Scottish clan warfare.

Saber...Curved sword with large hand-guard

Bludgeon.....................One- or two-handed club for whacking things

War hammer........Hammer with one blunt end and one spiked end

Pike.............Long, spearlike weapon used against cavalry assaults

Arbalest..................................Large, tremendously powerful crossbow

Flail..................Spiked metal ball(s) attached to a handle by a chain

Morning star............Pole with a spherical head with a large spike on its end and smaller spikes around its circumference

─────────"AX" ME NO MORE QUESTIONS─────────

When he was a boy, the person who became the first president of the United States allegedly cut down his father's cherry tree. The ax he used is on display in a museum, although, having had both its handle and head replaced several times, no part of the original ax remains.

─────────MAN-MADE OBJECTS LEFT ON MARS─────────

Mars 2..	USSR, 1971
Viking 1...	USA, 1976
Mars Pathfinder...	USA, 1997
Mars Polar Lander..	USA, 1999
Beagle 2...	Europe, 2003
MER B...	USA, 2004

> Spun sugar is called candy floss in the United Kingdom, *barbe à papa* in France, *zuckerwatte* in Germany, fairy floss in Australia, and cotton candy in the United States.

─────────PRO-WRESTLING MOVES─────────

Armbreaker • Atomic Drop
Powerslam • Twist of Fate
Brainbuster • Body Slam
Death Valley Driver
Russian Legsweep
Frankensteiner
Huracarrana
Irish Whip
Facebreaker
Electric Chair Bomb

---WEIRD WHISKER FACTS---

1. The average cat has 24 whiskers.

2. If the average man didn't shave, his beard could reach 13 feet.

3. Animal whiskers are called vibrissae.

4. Chinchilla whiskers are almost as long as their bodies.

5. Rats sometimes extend their whiskers sideways to stay balanced while they're swimming.

6. Walruses' whiskers can distinguish between two shapes as small as Skittles.

---ANIMAL SIXTH SENSE---

AMPULLAE OF LORENZI
This special organ enables sharks to detect weak electrical stimuli from the muscle movements of prey that are hidden or distant.

BUTTERFLY TARSI
The *tarsi*, or feet, of the American painted lady have special sensors that allow the butterfly to detect sweet food.

LATERAL LINE
Fish use this sense organ to detect changes in water pressure and feel the movement of other animals in the water nearby.

JACOBSON'S ORGAN
Snakes use this organ to "taste" prey. Their forked tongues collect chemicals from the air and bring them into the mouth, where the organ is located.

A hair transplant involves the removal of a patch of hairy scalp from the head. Hundreds of individual hairs or hair clusters are then taken from the patch under a magnifying glass and sewn back into the scalp to cover the bald area.

——————— AN ETHICAL PROBLEM ———————

A runaway train is hurtling toward five people tied to a railway track. You can save them by pulling a lever that steers the train down a branch line. Unfortunately, there is a single person tied to the branch line. Do you pull the lever?

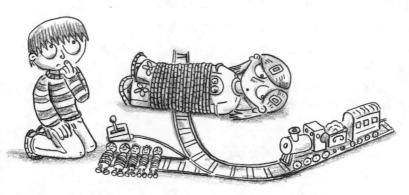

——————INTERNATIONAL DIALING CODES——————

Antarctica...+672

Australia..+61

France...+33

Germany..+49

Greece...+30

Italy...+39

Mongolia...+976

Netherlands...+31

Poland...+48

Spain...+34

Switzerland..+41

UK...+44

USA...+1

——————HOW TO INSULT SOMEONE AND——————
GET AWAY WITH IT

Memorize these handy put-downs, which you can use in all sorts of situations. Your family, friends, and teachers will be so amazed by your impressive vocabulary that you won't even get into trouble.

Abhorrent (ab-hor-uhnt)—disgusting:
"The state of my brother's bedroom is abhorrent."

Asinine (ass-ih-nine)—very stupid:
"That was an asinine thing to do."

Decrepit (di-krep-it)—very old and feeble:
"Teacher is so decrepit, I'm amazed he's still alive."

Disingenuous (dis-in-jen-yoo-uhs)—insincere, false:
"Your excuses are rather disingenuous."

Fatuous (fach-oo-uhs)—foolish:
"I am tired of your fatuous jokes."

Malevolent (muh-lev-uh-luhnt)—mean, spiteful:
"You are the most malevolent person in this school."

Malodorous (mal-oh-der-uhs)—smelly, stinky:
*"Your dog is the most malodorous thing
I have ever had the misfortune to encounter."*

Ninnyhammer (nin-ee-ham-er)—a fool:
"What a ninnyhammer my sister is!"

Puerile (pyoo-er-il)—childish, immature:
"That was such a puerile thing to say."

The Goliath bird-eating spider, a type of tarantula living in the South American jungle, is recorded as the world's biggest spider. It has a leg span of around 11 inches (28 cm).

GOOD-BYE

So long
Farewell
Cheerio
Ta-ta
See you later, alligator
In a while, crocodile